BLOOD RIVER

Falcon SAS Thrillers
Book One

Robert Charles

BLOOD RIVER

Published by Sapere Books.

20 Windermere Drive, Leeds, England, LS17 7UZ,
United Kingdom

saperebooks.com

ISBN: 978-1-80055-479-5

CHAPTER 1

The ambush was the first of many.

It was a rushed job, just a handful of men with automatic weapons, thrown into a hastily chosen position with a maximum of speed and a minimum of planning. It was a botched job before it started, and only with a lesser man for a target could it have had any hope of success.

But it was a sign, a grim omen of bigger and more bloody obstacles to follow. Somehow a hostile element from the other side had learned that the Falcon was coming, and they were determined to stop him.

The other side had many names and faces. They were the wolves and jackals of the world, the vultures and scavengers, and all those groups and organizations who found purpose and profit in preying on the innocent and the weak. They were the vicious, the corrupt, and the power-hungry.

They were organized big crime; the Mafia, the Triads, and all the other secret, criminal underworlds which plagued every modern society. More recently they had been joined and were fast being overshadowed by the even more ruthless terrorist organizations which had mushroomed all over the globe. Big crime sought the power that money could buy, while the terrorists sought their power more directly and more completely through political domination. But both sides used the same weapons of fear and violence, and both sides robbed, raped, plundered and exploited the same victims.

The other side were the Devil's spawn in the fertile fields of a troubled world. They were the predators, always ready to attack and feed upon the vast game herds of ordinary men and women who wanted only to be left to live out their lives in peace.

The other side was the unholy alliance of animal man: the brute forces within mankind who would trample and abuse the rest, rending mercilessly with tooth and claw to achieve their own selfish and greed-driven ends.

Mark Falcon had learned how to recognize the real enemies in a confused world where all too often race, religion or nationality were mistaken as the dividing lines. Falcon knew that good and evil existed in almost equal proportions in every colour and creed. Each had its own share of the unGodly.

But the other side had also learned to recognize and fear Mark Falcon.

They knew he was coming.

They intended to stop him.

Someone should have told them that the superb fighting machine and battle tactician, Falcon of the S.A.S., was virtually unstoppable.

The helicopter had landed ten minutes before, dropping out of the howling blackness of the storm-filled tropical night. The full fury of the elements had smashed into it on the last lap of the 370-mile flight from Brunei to Kuching, roaring up from the mountains and jungles of central Borneo to the south.

The wind had hit first, and then the near-solid wall of rain, a double hammer blow that had almost batted the chopper out of the sky. Somehow it had all held together. The rotor blades slicing through the vertical downpour had somehow stayed intact when they should have sheared off under the abnormal strain. And somehow the struggling, white-faced pilot had held his machine up under the onslaught.

The last few miles had been a miracle. The helicopter should have crashed into the tormented sea, or into the flailing palm trees that thrashed the twisting coastline. The storm threw it to and fro with Satanic glee, as easily and as carelessly as it chased the swirling palm fronds. For one heart-stopping moment they were within a hair's breadth of plunging into a jungle-covered headland, but the winds which seemed hell-bent on destroying the chopper suddenly gusted sideways and lifted them over. Foliage whipped at the undercarriage but failed to pull them down.

The flight controller at Kuching had talked them in to the airport, and the chopper had almost demolished the control tower for his pains. The large square, lighted windows had appeared with terrifying suddenness out of the violent blackness. The rain curtains had parted briefly to give a split-second warning and the pilot had yelled with alarm as he heaved back and twisted on the control column. The helicopter had jerked up and leaned sharply to starboard, and the rotor blades had whirled past within shaved inches of the shocked faces behind the windows.

After that the pilot put her down in a hurry, and he was lucky. The wind dropped by a few miles per hour and there were men waiting on the airfield to grab hold of the chopper and rope her down to steel spikes hammered quickly into the earth. The pilot switched off the engine with a huge sigh of relief, slumped thankfully in his seat and closed his eyes.

The helicopter carried one VIP passenger, a tall man with cool hazel eyes and dark blond hair. He wore a raincoat and hat but carried no luggage. The trip had been too urgent to waste time packing shirts. He smiled at the pilot and lightly punched the man's arm.

'Thanks, Jack. You flew it like an ace.'

The pilot slowly opened his eyes. Sweat drenched his face and his whole body felt like a limp rag. He was an American flying for one of the major oil companies drilling in the Brunei oil fields, and he had made the flight as a favour authorized by his top management.

He said with feeling. 'If I had known how rough it was gonna get at the finish I wouldn't have come. I sure hope it was necessary.'

Falcon chuckled. 'So do I.'

The pilot stared at him. The guy had sat calm all through. There wasn't a drop of sweat on him or a hair out of place, and now there wasn't even any aftermath reaction. And by the sound of it the guy didn't yet know why he had been summoned in such a hell of a hurry. Falcon was so cool it was unbelievable. He either had nerves of tempered steel or no nerves at all.

Headlights stabbed through the rain and a large black limousine pulled up close beside the helicopter. Falcon unbuckled his seat belt and stood up.

'It looks like someone is waiting for me.' He offered the pilot a handshake. 'Thanks for the ride, Jack. I'll look you up when I get back to Brunei. I figure I owe you a beer.'

The rear door of the limousine opened as Falcon exited from the helicopter and dived through the rain. He plunged inside, hanging on to his hat, and an arm reached past him to slam the door shut again. The big car moved off immediately.

The car was chauffeur-driven, and Falcon had noted the sodden Union Jack plastered tight around the miniature flag mast on the long bonnet. The man who shared the back seat wore the essential hat and raincoat. His face was young and serious, and trying hard to look older and relaxed. He introduced himself as Bill Hollis from the British Consulate in Kuching.

'Sorry about the awful panic,' Hollis apologized. 'And the absolutely awful weather. The monsoon seems to have arrived early this year. My — er — Head of Department is waiting for you,' he added awkwardly.

Falcon noted the hesitation over a title but restrained a smile. 'Where?' he asked.

'On a warship,' Hollis said vaguely. 'In the harbour.'

Falcon was intrigued, but Hollis was uncomfortable, as though he didn't know how much talk was allowed. He was also a very junior diplomat, probably with more questions in his head than answers, so Falcon let the issue rest. He guessed that he was going to find out what it was all about soon enough.

In any event it was already obvious that he was in for another scary ride. The Malayan chauffeur had his foot flat to the floor, despite the fact that his headlights could only penetrate for a few yards through the pouring black cataract that filled the night. Even at ground level the storm-force winds were strong enough to bowl the car off the road, which was littered with broken palm fronds and other debris.

Despite some wild skids on the muddy surface they survived the fast drive from the airport into town, where their driver at last slowed up a little. Falcon had a rain-blurred impression of an untidy sprawl of shack-like houses, roofed with corrugated tin sheeting, which gradually gave way to more solid brick buildings and shops in the town centre. He knew that in daylight and without the torrential rain the streets would be teeming with the local population, but right now they were eerily deserted.

Well, almost.

Because right then they ran into the ambush.

The set-up was a simple one, just a car and a battered, canvas-hooded truck parked nose to nose and blocking off the full width of the road. There were half a dozen men behind the barricade, split into groups of three on each sidewalk. They all carried submachine guns.

Falcon's combat training evaluated the situation instantly as it appeared. The chauffeur swore as he saw the obstacle and his foot stamped down hard on the brake. The big limousine immediately slewed sideways into another skid.

Falcon yelled a warning as he hooked an iron arm around Hollis's shoulders, and as he ducked he heaved Hollis down onto the floor of the car beside him. The submachine guns poured a fusillade of bullets through the windows, smothering them with broken glass and great splashes of crimson blood. The unlucky chauffeur had been blasted into the front passenger seat, and with the top of his head and half his face shredded away he had died instantly.

Falcon was already moving, following the reflex instinct of a man who automatically made himself the master of any battlefield. His 20-20 vision needed only one lightning scan, and he had memorized every rain-streaked detail in the split second before he had ducked. Now that brief glimpse was a battle plan frozen on to his brain, and he knew that the best act of defence was always to attack.

He was unarmed, so the only weapon he had was the car itself. He reached through the front seats, up to the wheel, and pulled it hard to the right. The battle plan had showed the brick wall of a building behind the sidewalk on that side — and one of the ambush team moving out from the barricade to gain an unrestricted field of fire.

There was a jolt as the front wheels mounted the kerb, a thud and a shriek of agony as the bonnet splattered something yielding and soft, and then a terrific, bone-jarring crash as the vehicle hit into the solid brick wall. There were no windows left to break, but the ruptured metal shrieked as it ripped and crumpled, drowning the more frail human sound in the explosion of impact.

Falcon pushed his door open and dived through it, throwing himself low and rolling fast over the rain-hammered sidewalk. The car had brought down half the wall and crushed one of the enemy. The man was draped over the bonnet and half buried under the collapsed brickwork, and as the dust settled around him he expired and his hands opened to let the submachine gun he carried slide over the buckled wing of the car to clatter onto the sidewalk.

With the speed of a striking mamba Falcon changed direction and pulled himself toward the fallen weapon.

Surprise was now Falcon's. The other side had not expected anyone to emerge alive from the wreckage, much less to come out fast and fighting.

There were two of the enemy left on this side of the road, both Malays. One was a thin youth with spectacles and a red headband. The other had a lean face and gold teeth.

Gold-teeth reacted first, bringing his weapon up again and running out from behind the barricade to fire a burst. He was too hasty and the rain driving into his face was blinding him. He missed completely and the spray of bullets did no more than chew up the sidewalk where Falcon had been a second before.

Then Falcon had his hands on the dropped submachine gun, and Falcon did not miss.

An accurate scythe of bullets stitched up Gold-teeth from hip to shoulder, flinging him lifeless into the middle of the road. The guy with the red headband was trying to grab a piece of the action but Falcon was again rolling clear and he couldn't get an aimed shot. He was weaving in agitation behind the barricade when Falcon fired his next burst beneath the truck and cut his legs off at the ankles.

It was all too much for the second half of the ambush team on the opposite side of the road. They stared for one horrified moment at the carnage, and then their collective nerve broke and all three of them turned and fled.

Falcon checked out both sides of the barricade, satisfying himself that there was no more danger. Then he straightened up. The enemy had vanished into the storm-lashed night. They were on their home ground and he was a stranger here, so he didn't attempt to follow.

Now the echoes of gunfire had faded there was no sound except the falling rain and the hiss of steam from the smashed radiator of the car. Then he heard a bang and a scrape from the far side.

He walked round the car. Bill Hollis had pushed open the rear door on the other side and fell out in an awkward heap at his feet. The young man was white and shaken, but he was fumbling bravely inside his raincoat and finally succeeded in extracting a snagged 0.32 automatic from the shoulder holster under his armpit.

'It's okay,' Falcon said calmly. 'I don't think you'll need it now.'

He scanned the battlefield again, the seemingly casual but infinitely careful double-check of a man who knew how to stay alive. Then he continued: 'But I'm beginning to believe it is important that I get to this meeting with your boss. Have a look round and see if you can find us a cab.'

CHAPTER 2

They moved quickly away from the battlefield to avoid any delay with the local law, and after a quarter mile and a few twists and turns Hollis found a telephone and called up a cab. They reached the harbour and found a Royal Navy launch waiting for them at the quayside.

The warship proved to be the destroyer *Scotsman*, anchored a mile downriver toward the sea. Getting to her was another wild ride over the wind-tossed waters with the launch bucking and twisting like a rodeo bull beneath them. The rain still fell in solid sheets and the spray flew, but the rain had already done its worst and Hollis and Falcon were already as wet as they could possibly be.

They boarded the destroyer and were immediately taken to the officer's wardroom. Three men and a woman were already present, seated in comfortable armchairs, with drinks close to hand. The Commander of the *Scotsman* was easily identified by his gold braid and uniform. A younger man who wore the uniform of a Lieutenant in the British Army had parked himself close, but not too close, to the girl. The third man was in his fifties, grey-haired and showing signs of worry and strain. He rose to his feet and offered a hand of welcome.

'Captain Falcon, it was good of you to come at such short notice and at such speed. I'm John Norville.'

The Head of Bill Hollis's Department, Falcon deduced, still undefined. However, Norville held himself like an ex-Army man, and probably fronted as a military attaché to the consulate. Falcon shook hands as Norville quickly introduced the others.

'Captain Bartlett. The Navy are giving us full cooperation with this job. It's a godsend that they were on hand when it happened.'

'Our role is shrinking,' Bartlett said wryly. 'But we still have a duty to protect a few out-of-the-way places like Brunei. We were on a short patrol at sea, and fortunately within a few hours sailing distance of Kuching.'

'Lieutenant Peter Kennard,' Norville continued. 'And Doctor Gail Crawford. They'll be going with you, so you'll have plenty of time to get to know each other over the next few days.'

Falcon acknowledged them in turn, then looked to Norville to ask exactly where they were all going. But Norville had momentarily lost his poise and looked awkward.

'Er — by the way — do you have some identification, Captain Falcon?'

Bill Hollis went pink at the cheeks. He had forgotten to check. Falcon smiled and offered his passport.

Norville flipped over the pages and still looked faintly uncertain.

'Is this all?'

Falcon nodded. 'I'm not officially with S.I.S or M.I.6. Technically I am just what it says on my passport, a journalist.' He smiled briefly. 'But for fifteen years I served with the S.A.S. In those days I learned a lot, and I've forgotten nothing. I don't know yet what you want from me, but I know where you got my name, and how you knew that I was available. You were advised by Harry Killian.'

'Of course,' Norville smiled to make amends. 'Good old Harry. I served with him in France.'

'I don't think so,' Falcon contradicted him politely. 'Colonel Killian served in Italy and Greece, Malaya, Aden and Oman, and here in Borneo. But to the best of my knowledge he never saw any action in France.'

Now Norville looked genuinely apologetic. 'You are exactly right, Captain Falcon. It was bad form for me to play games. I assure you I have no more doubts.'

Borneo, Aden and Oman, they had been Falcon's theatres of war also, with the added dimension of two duty tours in the bitter and bloodily divided streets of Northern Ireland. He had learned all the arts of jungle and desert and street warfare and survival the hard way, by repeated practical experience under fire with the toughest and most efficient fighting force the world had ever known. The Special Air Service Regiment, formed out of necessity during the dark days of World War Two, had become the elite, tactical spearhead in every campaign that Britain had fought since. It had also become a crack anti-terrorist unit, on call at a moment's notice, ready to go anywhere in the world, to perform any task of military surgery with all the precision of a finely-honed scalpel.

For fifteen years Mark Falcon had been one of those unknown heroes. He was a first-class marksman and familiar with all types of NATO and Communist Bloc small arms. He had undergone intensive training in unarmed combat, parachute jumping, underwater sabotage, and the knowledge and use of all types of explosives. Like every other S.A.S. trooper before and after him he had been moulded into the ultimate human weapon, toughened by the most rigorous training programmes and gruelling route marches, until he was capable of an instant, deadly response to any emergency, even in a state of near exhaustion.

However, Mark Falcon had learned more than just military tactics and skills, he had also learned a whole lot more about himself. He had tested and trained his body to its physical limits as a fighter and soldier, but he had also been doubly blessed with a highly intelligent mind. He had taken degrees in history and politics before joining the army, and he continued to read widely on every subject under the sun. He had an obsession for knowledge, and he was striving to fully understand his world, himself, and his fellow man. He began to realize that although the role of a soldier was essential to the defence of freedom and right, it was often only essential because the politicians had failed. He also realized that the world was too wide and complex, with far too much to be seen and learned, for him to confine himself to the limited life of soldiering.

The turning point in Falcon's career came during the five-year campaign in Oman. Perhaps it was ordained, for the chain of events began with his first meeting with Colonel Harry Killian.

Killian was one of the founder members and guiding lights of the S.A.S. A veteran of World War Two he had been involved with the regiment from its very beginning. Events in Oman, a rugged mountain and desert sultanate on the Persian Gulf, vital for the strategic control of the Hormuz Strait and the free flow of Middle East oil, were not going well for the sultan and his British allies. The communist-led rebel tribesmen were not being beaten. They were stubborn and brave, the terrain was on their side, and the war was dragging on. Killian was sent out to evaluate the situation, and decide if any change of focus was needed.

For Harry Killian a comfortable debate on theory in the safety of base HQ, and then a quick flight out again, was definitely not enough. He wanted to visit the front line, to give the troops a pep talk and a morale boost, and a chance to tell him face to face why they thought they were not winning the war. He set out in a Land Rover with a trooper driver, and Captain Mark Falcon detailed as his guide and escort.

On the way they ran into an ambush. The Land Rover was blown up as it passed over a mine, somersaulted three times and burst into flames. The driver was killed instantly. Harry Killian had his right arm blown off and lost his right eye. Mark Falcon suffered a six-inch shrapnel gash in his left thigh, multiple cuts, burns and bruises, and two broken ribs.

To finish off the job a six strong group of hostile tribesmen charged the burning vehicle with rifles and knives.

But the job was never finished. Falcon had dragged Killian clear of the flames and then opened fire with a sterling submachine gun. He had killed three of the enemy. The others retreated.

Falcon had stopped his own bleeding and then bound up the stump of Killian's arm. He had dragged the colonel into the sparse shelter of an outcrop of sun-baked rocks, and held the position for a further six hours. Despite the sweltering heat and his loss of blood, and despite the fact that the enemy had been doubled by reinforcements and he was down to his last handful of bullets, he was still alive when an S.A.S. patrol at last came in search of the overdue Land Rover. So was Harry Killian, but only just.

Falcon spent the next two months in hospital, and in an ironic way the ambush that almost killed him had also saved his life. During his absence his fifteen-man troop, commanded by another officer, had been flown up to a mountain-top position in a helicopter which had come under fire from a heavy machine gun. The helicopter had crashed and every man aboard had been killed.

For Falcon it was a cruel blow. Except for the officer who had taken his place he had known every one of those men closer than a brother. They had trained together, fought together, slept together and sweated and bled together. He had led them through a score of battles in three campaigns. They had called him 'Skipper', and he would gladly have given his own life in place of any one of them. In one foul stroke he had lost virtually every true friend he ever had.

He did not realize it at the time, but he had gained another.

He had recovered from his wounds, but he was not fated to fight again in Oman. After a period of rest and leave he had returned to active service again in Northern Ireland. However, he no longer had any heart for teamwork. The old camaraderie had been something very special, something unique, almost a form of communal marriage. There was no way he could rebuild it again, and it would have been a form of sacrilege to let any other group of men call him 'Skipper.' He had volunteered instead for undercover assignments, and worked alone.

He proved to himself on those last dangerous anti-terrorist missions that he had not lost his nerve, and then he had resigned his commission. During his enforced idleness in hospital he had discovered he had another talent, the ability to write, and so he had chosen a profession that enabled him to roam at will the world he found so fascinating. His reputation as an author and journalist was promptly established with his first book; a study of guerrilla and terrorist aims and tactics throughout the world. The first English language printing had been bought up almost entirely by the army, police and intelligence establishments, and it had immediately become a classic textbook.

From there he had gone on to become a freelance correspondent for *International Geographic*, a magazine specializing in international news, political and travel features. Since then he had written up and photographed virtually every remote or spectacular feature of the earth's surface, and had covered every brushfire war in Africa, Asia and Latin America over the past decade.

Inevitably his instinct for a story and the lure of danger had led him into crisis situations, and inevitably destiny had not intended that those unique warrior skills he had acquired during his military career should go to waste. All too often he was the right man in a position where his particular abilities were desperately needed, and it only needed the right man to recognize those fortuitous circumstances and point him in the right direction.

The man who aimed Falcon was Harry Killian. With only one arm and one eye Killian was no longer fit for any form of active service, but he still had invaluable practical experience and a brilliant guiding brain. He now worked behind a Whitehall desk in the shadowy world of Britain's Secret Intelligence Service, and frequently found that when some world trouble spot erupted, Falcon was already there, available with impeccable and genuine cover, and never hesitant to respond to a just cause.

Falcon had been engaged on a feature story on the Brunei oil fields for *International Geographic* when this particular call had reached him. There had been no details, just the indication that the call had originated from Whitehall.

To Falcon Whitehall meant Harry Killian, and that was enough.

He was needed in Kuching.

Urgently.

So here he had come.

'You're soaked,' Bartlett observed, looking with some distaste at the pools of rainwater dripping on to his dark blue wardroom carpet. 'I can find you a change of clothes. My first officer is about your height and weight.'

'Later perhaps,' Falcon politely postponed the offer as he put aside his raincoat. 'First I think I'd rather find out why I'm here?'

'A drink then?' Bartlett was determined to show some hospitality.

Falcon accepted a whisky, and then sat down to face Norville.

'We have a problem,' the man from the consulate began quietly. 'At two o'clock this afternoon a chartered airliner took off from Manilla, heading for Djakarta. The flight route took it over central Borneo, and that's where it had the damned bad luck to run into this hurricane that is now playing havoc with the whole of the north coast.'

'The plane has crashed,' Falcon guessed without difficulty.

Norville nodded. 'We know it's down and we know roughly where. The pilot managed to get out a mayday and his position before he crashed. There was no word after the crash, so we don't know if there was any fire, or if it exploded on impact. We don't even know if any of them are still alive, but we have to hope they are and we have to find out fast. These are very important people.'

'How important?'

'They are all top-rank United Nations diplomats. Four Asians: Doctor Sumantri from Indonesia, Shinawatra from Thailand, Moreno from the Philippines, and an Indian woman,

21

Kamala Chavan. There was also a top US State Department official on board, Sam Jordan.'

Falcon nodded thoughtfully. 'As you say, Very Important People. I understand they were on a peace mission.'

'That's right. Brunei is due for full independence, and we're all afraid the event is going to leave a political vacuum in this part of the world. The UN team were looking for peace guarantees in all the South East Asia capitals: Singapore, Bangkok, Kuala Lumpur, Manilla and Djakarta. They were hoping to ensure some sort of stability in the area.'

'It's not the political vacuum they are afraid of,' Bartlett clarified carefully. 'The Sultan of Brunei is a bit of the autocratic old school, but his rule is stable enough. It's more a problem of a military vacuum. At the moment Brunei is protected by a battalion of Gurkhas under British officers. When the state becomes independent they will have to be withdrawn. Then Brunei and its rich oil fields will become an open target to outside aggression.'

'Specifically, terrorist attacks,' Norville concluded. 'It could be internal. We know more than thirty of Brunei's most militant students have received training and indoctrination in Libya. Or it could be an overspill of terrorism from Indonesia or the Philippines. Brunei is going to be the soft spot that could make a useful base.'

Falcon understood the situation, for it formed part of the background to the story he had been writing. Terrorism was an international web with strands woven in all directions, so any unprotected spot on the map was a source of potential worry for the entire area.

He said grimly, 'I know the UN team had hopes of getting the nearer South East Asia governments to promise some support for Brunei. Especially an assurance from the

Federation of Malaysia that their Sabah and Sarawak borders with Brunei would be adequately policed to stop any hostile infiltration. How much success were they getting?'

Norville shrugged. 'We don't know. It's too soon in the tour and they haven't issued any statements. Our main concern right now is that the plane has crashed into some of the most remote and inaccessible mountain and jungle country on God's earth. Sam Jordan is on board, and practically all the local politicians who are genuinely committed to peaceful co-existence in this part of Asia. We have to pray that most of them are still alive. And somehow we have to reach them and bring them back.'

'I take it that any hope of an air search and rescue is out.'

Norville nodded. 'The hurricane has moved up fast. You only just made your flight along the north coast. South of here the whole of central Borneo is being ravaged by monsoon storms. It could be days before the bad weather clears, maybe weeks. As soon as it breaks we'll launch an air search, but we can't afford to wait. In the meantime we have to start another approach — and that's where you come in.'

He looked uncertainly into the cool hazel eyes of his only hope. 'I don't understand your exact status, Captain. You've told me you are not a direct agent of any of our intelligence services, so it would seem that I can't give you any direct orders. However, Harry Killian does seem to have unlimited faith in you. Immediately this situation was known in Whitehall your name was flashed back to me as the one man close at hand with all the necessary qualifications to lead a rescue mission.'

Falcon smiled. 'So let's just leave it at that. Tell me what you have in mind for this alternative approach.'

Norville looked as though he would have been happier with a more official basis for Falcon's presence, but there was enough relief in him to refrain from looking a gift horse in the mouth.

'There is only one way,' he explained. 'The rescue mission has to go upriver from the south coast. The river routes are the only way to penetrate the interior, and they all flow down from the central mountains and out to sea. It's everybody's bad luck that the plane crashed on the south side of the mountains.'

Falcon frowned. 'From here the south coast is a long haul.'

'Approximately six hundred sea miles,' Bartlett confirmed calmly. 'That's about fifteen hours, and my Executive officer had orders to get under way the moment you stepped on board.'

'This is where we owe thanks to the Navy,' Norville acknowledged. 'This destroyer is going to be your ferry boat to the river mouth.'

'But it won't get up the river,' Falcon said wryly.

'Again it's hats off to the Navy. They're providing an SRN5 military hovercraft. That's where Lieutenant Kennard comes in — he's your pilot/commander. He'll get you as far up that godforsaken river as any craft can go. And you'll have half a dozen Gurkha troops to back you up.'

Falcon looked at Kennard and approved of what he saw. If he had to have a team then this so far silent but solid and confident looking young soldier appeared a good type to have along. Kennard had blue eyes and light blond hair. His smile was almost boyish as he raised one hand in casual salute. Falcon returned the smile.

Bartlett said quietly. 'You don't owe us anything, John. The Navy has been nursing this part of the world for a long time. It's all part of the job, and we have no desire to see all our efforts go to waste and ruin as soon as we have to finally pull out. I'm as concerned to get that UN peace team back and continuing their mission as you are.'

Falcon was looking at the girl. She was about twenty-eight, tall with long, lovely legs neatly crossed as she leaned back in her chair. She wore an open-neck white shirt and dark skirt. Her hair was a rich chestnut red, pulled back and tied practically at the nape of her neck with a yellow band. Her eyes were a striking honey brown with a hint of sleeping fire.

'Where does Doctor Crawford fit in?' He asked.

'There are two women on that crashed plane,' Norville told him. 'Mrs Chavan, the Indian delegate. And Sumantri had his young wife with him. She's eight months pregnant. You're going to need a doctor, and in the circumstances a woman doctor fits the bill.'

'Don't worry about me,' Gail Crawford assured him. 'I've been working up-country for the World Health Organization for the past eight months. I'm acclimatized. I can rough it.'

CHAPTER 3

Norville was startled when they told him about the attack on the way from the airport. His face went pale.

'Dear Lord,' he groaned. 'How on earth—?'

'I've been thinking about it,' Bill Hollis offered. 'There must have been an information leak for them to know that Captain Falcon was coming. And the only people who knew were ourselves and the airport authorities. Obviously the helicopter pilot or his head office must have filed some kind of flight plan, and of course we had to smooth customs and immigration at this end. Somewhere in one of those areas, somebody made a telephone call.'

'But who? Why? And who to?'

'I think Bill is probably right,' Falcon said calmly. 'And the answers to all your questions can only be the KGB. I guess they must have a *residentura* here in Kuching?'

'Pitkov!' Norville was no longer baffled. 'The Mongolian Weasel!'

'So let's fit it together the way Pitkov must have done. I take it the plane crash is no secret?'

'It was broadcast on the local radio.'

'And the arrival of this destroyer is also no secret. Anyone with eyes can see her. *Scotsman*'s presence must be a bit unusual now that Britain no longer has any direct responsibility for Sarawak, so your friend Pitkov must have been burning with curiosity. Then his tip-off man at the airport tells him that the British consulate have yelled for help to someone named Mark Falcon. So he immediately looks up that name in his files—'

Falcon paused and made a regretful shrug of his shoulders. 'Unfortunately I tangled with the KGB *residentura* in Macao a couple of years ago. The KGB are always suspicious of journalists, even though most of them are totally innocent of any intelligence connections, so it is possible that they have circulated a file with my name. It will have more guesswork than real details, but it could be enough to give Pitkov some clues.'

'If he owns a pair of binoculars he would also be able to identify the SRN5 lashed to my aft deck,' Bartlett added grimly. 'It all adds up to a rescue mission to be led by Captain Falcon.'

'So Pitkov decides to take no chances and calls up a local hit team,' Hollis concluded, with some satisfaction at having provided the answer.

'Obviously he doesn't want the diplomats on that plane to survive.' Falcon frowned thoughtfully. 'When I get there I think I'll take the time for a close look at the wreckage. It might be interesting to know the exact cause of the crash.'

Norville was again shocked. He hadn't thought beyond the weather and suddenly it was much more complicated. 'You think sabotage?'

'I'll tell you when I get back,' Falcon promised. 'Right now I'd like to take a look at the map and see the exact location where the plane went down.'

Bartlett had a map already opened out on a side table. It showed Borneo and the surrounding South China, Java and Celebes seas. They had all been studying it before Falcon arrived.

'We're here,' Norville touched a finger on Kuching, the capital of Sarawak on the north east coast of the huge island. The top third of the island was divided into the Malaysian states of Sarawak and Sabah, and the small British protectorate of Brunei tucked between the two. The rest of the island bore the name Kalimantan, which was Indonesian Borneo.

Norville's finger moved diagonally, south-east across the map, crossing the Sarawak–Kalimantan border and the southern spur of the central mountains. It stopped at the headwaters of one of the dozen rivers that flowed out into the Java Sea, where a cross had been marked in red ink.

'This is where the plane went down. Three hundred miles in a straight line, but more than twice as far the way you have to travel.'

Peter Kennard had moved up behind them. 'Captain Bartlett has estimated fifteen hours to get down to the river mouth. After that we've got to get about eighty miles up the river, so I would estimate another three or four hours. The SRN5 can do 70 miles per hour, but of course we can't hope to maintain that all the way.'

'How much do you know about the river?'

'It's called the Kiamba. There's a town called Batakan situated at the river mouth, and a place called Surajong about forty miles upstream.' Kennard had obviously done some hasty homework.

'How far is it navigable?'

'There's a river boat of some sort that plods between Batakan and Surajong about once a month, and anything any boat can do a hovercraft can do better. After that I don't know. We'll slow down, but we can skim over sandbanks and minor rapids, so I'm hoping we'll get right up to the crash area.'

Falcon nodded approval and looked back to Norville. 'Have we got clearance from the Indonesian Government?'

Norville looked uncomfortable. 'Our people in Djakarta are working on it, but by the time anything gets relayed to Batakan

28

it will probably be too late for anybody on that plane. I'm afraid the idea is for you to nip in quick and get them out, and hopefully we'll be able to tidy up the formalities later.'

'*Scotsman* will back off to sea and wait for you,' Bartlett said from his chair. 'When you come back downriver just send us a radio signal and we'll move in again to rendezvous and pick you all up.'

He made it sound as though it was going to be smooth and easy, but Falcon had a gut feeling that didn't agree. He remembered the three men he had been obliged to kill, and that was before the real job had even started.

The destroyer slowed before it left the Kuching River for the open sea, just long enough for Norville and Hollis to disembark and hitch a ride back to town with the pilot boat.

They left with gloomy faces. The return trip meant getting wet and more joyless discomfort, and at the end of it there was an embarrassing mess to be cleared up with the local police. A dead chauffeur was pointing a trail back to the British Consulate, and the two diplomats had a joint headache in deciding how they were going to explain it all away.

Falcon had to concede it was now their problem. His own lay ahead up the Kiamba River.

It was now almost dawn and he accepted the offer of a few hours sleep before breakfast. A bunk was found for him in one of the officers' cabins, and after a quick shower he turned in. The *Scotsman* pitched and rolled heavily as she battled her way as fast as possible through the massive, storm-whipped seas, but after the helicopter flight the ship seemed safe and solid and Falcon slept soundly.

The destroyer rounded Cape Datu and swung south-west, finally turning her bows to plunge due south down into the

Java Sea. The bad weather continued and when Falcon awoke the ship was still sliding and rolling and the storm was still raging.

Falcon showered again, dressed in the dry clothes that had been found to fit him, and went back to the wardroom.

He found Kennard sitting at the cleared breakfast table with a short, stocky man in the uniform of a British sergeant. They broke off their conversation as Falcon came in.

'Meet Tom Harris.' Kennard introduced his companion. 'Tom's my co-pilot/navigator/radio operator/maintenance engineer — you name it, if it needs doing on the SRN5, Tom does it.'

Harris stood up and they shook hands.

'I can recommend the eggs and bacon, sir. Not bad for the Navy.' Harris chanced a smile. 'If the old stomach's not too poorly.'

'It's a civilian stomach,' Falcon confessed. 'But I think it can stand up to bacon and eggs.' He nodded to the attending steward and added. 'An orange juice first and coffee to follow.'

'Tom and I have worked together for a couple of years,' Kennard confided. 'We play about mostly around the Brunei coast, just to keep our hand in. At other times the Navy ferries us around as part of their patrols. We're officially attached to the Gurkha battalion in Brunei, but like them we're a bit of a leftover really, the rearguard of a retreating empire. Until this job came along I was beginning to think we were wasting our time.'

'I did my first duty tour out here in the mid-sixties,' Harris said. 'During confrontation — that's what they called the war between Malaysia and Indonesia. Before Lieutenant Kennard's time, but then we had a real job to do, patrolling the

Indonesian coastline to stop old Sukarno's sampan raiders making their hit and run attacks on North Borneo.'

'Sarawak and Sabah were British protectorates then,' Kennard explained. 'The Indonesians objected when they achieved independence and chose to join the Federation of Malaysia. Brunei was scheduled to join with the other two, but the old Sultan changed his mind at the last moment.'

'I remember it well,' Falcon said with a brief smile. 'I saw my first action with the S.A.S. here in Borneo.'

'Did you now.' Kennard looked at Falcon with new respect.

'I've heard some tales about your mob,' Harris said in the same tone.

'Some of them could have been exaggerated,' Falcon demurred. 'Tell me about your hovercraft.'

'It's a lovely vehicle, sir.' Harris was enthusiastic. 'It'll go almost anywhere. They've brought out a bigger version now, the SRN6, but give me the old Mark 5 any day. It's big enough, and it's ideal for where we're going. In the old days the Navy used to patrol the Java Sea with minesweepers. Sukarno's boys used to waltz their way right through them — those sampans were pretty nippy with their auxiliary engines — but they couldn't outrun the old SRN5!'

'How well do you know the Kiamba?' Falcon asked as he began his breakfast.

'I don't, sir. But these coastlines are pretty much alike, all swampy river deltas, dotted with hundreds of sandbars and little jungle islands. Out here when you've seen one river you've seen them all.'

He paused, then added. 'It's a pity the weather's so rough on top, sir. We could give you a preview of the SRN5.'

Falcon smiled, for it was obvious that Harris was one of those born mechanics who pursued a long-standing love affair with his chosen machine.

'I guess I'll get to know her soon enough,' he promised.

'In the meantime you may as well get acquainted with the rest of the expedition,' Kennard decided. 'When you've eaten we'll take you aft to meet the Gurkhas.'

There were six of the sturdy little Nepalese, all of them smartly kitted out in crisp khaki shorts, shirts and jungle hats. They had gathered in the crew's mess room which they had to themselves, and like off-duty soldiers of any race they were playing cards. Their N.C.O. snapped them briskly to attention as Falcon, Kennard and Harris entered.

Kennard put them at ease. 'Sergeant Bahadur Rama,' he said, indicating the fierce little man with three arm stripes and a black moustache. 'Fifteen years' service with the British Army.'

'I've worked before with Gurkhas,' Falcon said with approval. 'I've always found them to be first-class soldiers.'

Bahadur Rama beamed at the compliment, his teeth flashing brilliant white.

A thin, wiry Gurkha with two stripes was Corporal Ganju, ten years' service and an equally happy smile when the point was made. The four private soldiers were younger men, but looked well trained and efficient. Their relationship with Kennard was respectful but comfortable, which was a point to the lieutenant. He was young, but he had to be a competent officer to stand well with men like these. Falcon guessed that Kennard would probably have been entrusted to handle this mission alone if the lives involved had not been political dynamite.

They stayed for half an hour, getting to know each other, and eventually Bahadur Rama seized upon a chance glance by Falcon at one of the heavy kukri knives which all the Gurkhas wore in polished black leather scabbards.

'You want to see, sah!'

Without waiting for any further prompting the Gurkha sergeant proudly drew the wide, curved blade and offered it for inspection.

'It's primarily a chopping weapon,' Kennard contributed as Falcon weighed the weapon in his hand. 'You probably know that with one blow they can slice the head off a bullock. I believe they still do it as part of their religious ceremonies in Nepal.'

'Also very good for cutting heads off enemies,' Bahadur Rama grinned. 'My father was sergeant in Burma in Great War. Cut off heads of many Japanese.' He saw Kennard's sharp frown and added regretfully. 'Not permitted now. All very bad thing.'

Falcon was not sure whether the words meant that it was a bad thing that Japanese heads had been lopped off in the past, or a bad thing that such activities were no longer permitted. He returned the kukri without comment.

Bahadur Rama carefully ran one brown thumb along the razor-edged blade, just enough to draw a minute trickle of red. Satisfied, he returned the kukri to its scabbard, and sucked briefly on his thumb to close the tiny wound.

Falcon knew it was all part of the ritual. Once the kukri was drawn honour demanded that the blade must taste blood before it went back into the scabbard.

He also knew that the ferocious reputation of these tough little fighting men was nothing less than the truth, and it was reassuring to know that they were all on the same side.

The weather conditions stayed bad over the next twelve hours as the destroyer slogged ever southward through the gale-force winds and mountainous seas. Finally, by late afternoon, she was able to change course to head due east along the south coast of Borneo. The weather improved, but it had already delayed them more than Bartlett had anticipated and it was nightfall again when they reached the mouth of the Kiamba River.

Bartlett called a last-minute briefing in the wardroom while the SRN5 was made ready. The latest radio reports showed that the monsoon storms were still raging over all of north and central Borneo. There was still no immediate hope of an air search, so the mission was go.

'You won't find them in the dark,' Bartlett apologized. 'But I can get you off at the crack of dawn.'

'Sooner by two or three hours,' Falcon decided. 'I'd like to get past those two towns — Batakan and Surajong — at night. It's the easiest way to avoid complications. After that we can wait for daylight to tackle the upper reaches of the river and make the actual search.'

'No problem,' Kennard said calmly. 'We know there are no major obstacles before Surajong, so we can cover the lower part of the river at night. We've buggered about on night exercises before, so we might as well have a go at the real thing.'

'Be just like old times,' Harris added complacently.

'Spare me from schoolboy heroes,' Gail Crawford said. But she was smiling and as keen to go as the rest of them.

Four hours later the hovercraft was launched and speeding rapidly over the last few sea miles to the darkened swamps of the river delta.

CHAPTER 4

Ragged gaps had broken through the cloud cover and there was some starlight but no moon as the SRN5 skimmed over the black waves. She rode smooth and buoyant on the cushion of air beneath her flexible armoured skirts. Her power came from a gas turbine engine driving her four-blade rotor propeller, and she maintained an easy 30 mph. It was less than half her full speed but Kennard was taking no unnecessary risks in the unfamiliar waters.

The interior of the hovercraft bore some resemblance to the flight deck and passenger cabin of a small aircraft. The control panel was a similar array of dials, switches and indicators, while the control column differed from an aircraft column in having a twist grip hand throttle instead of the usual half wheel. Opening the throttle increased the engine speed and the speed of the lift fan, giving the necessary lift control. Moving the control column forward or back controlled the pitch of the propeller blades, giving the vehicle forward or reverse momentum and controlling its speed.

Kennard's role as commander was nearer to that of a pilot than anything else, for his craft was airborne in motion. However, the fact that it travelled only a few feet above the surface of the sea meant that he had to combine many of the skills of seamanship.

Tom Harris sat in the navigation seat on Kennard's left-hand side, a chart spread out on his knees which he constantly checked with the radar screen in front of him. As yet they had not switched on the searchlight and were making their approach in darkness.

Falcon shared a double seat behind Kennard with Gail Crawford. Behind them sat the Gurkhas, stolid and patient, each of them armed with a Sterling submachine gun.

There were ten empty seats; one each for the six VIPs and the four plane crew they hoped to bring back.

Falcon was well satisfied with his team, and thought fleetingly that if any one of them was superfluous to the mission it was probably himself. Then he remembered the ambush in Kuching. There were people in this part of the world who didn't want the rescue mission to succeed, so perhaps he would be needed after all.

It was another reason why he had decided it might be wise to pass the river towns in darkness.

Kennard chatted cheerfully at the controls, explaining what he was doing and how the craft operated. It was mostly for Gail's benefit and she was sufficiently intrigued to keep him prompted with questions. Kennard was obviously pleased by her interest, and Falcon felt a faint twinge of jealousy.

There had been time throughout the long, waiting hours of the afternoon to get to know Gail Crawford. She was an American from the east coast and had worked in a Philadelphia hospital before joining the World Health Organization. Falcon had found himself liking her immediately as he listened to her talk. She was an intelligent woman who obviously had a great deal of compassion for the poorer peoples of the world. Anger flashed in her eyes when she spoke of their primitive living conditions, and the toll of death and disease caused by the lack of sanitation and proper medical services. She had wanted to help, and after eight months in the jungle villages of Sarawak she wanted to do more.

She was especially fond of babies. Her smile warmed when she talked of her health work with children, or else her eyes showed sharper anger when she spoke of their problems.

Falcon formed the impression of a determined and resourceful young woman, probably from a comfortable family background, who felt that she owed something to those who had been born less fortunate than herself.

He was also aware of her sexually. Her long legs were beautiful, her body was desirable, and the thought of that rich chestnut hair loosened and spilled wildly over a white pillow was almost erotic.

Kennard was even more badly smitten, and his boyish enthusiasm showed. Listening to the younger man eagerly describing the functions of his tailplane, trimmer control, and the pedal-operated rudder control bar caused Falcon to smile inwardly at his own moment of envy. He hoped he hadn't been so obvious.

Kennard could have her attention for now. On this trip competition would be pointless, and complications were unwanted, because there wasn't going to be time for anything other than the job at hand.

But later — when they got back to Kuching.

Then, hopefully, there would be time. And Gail Crawford would be well worth it.

'Two degrees to starboard, sir,' Tom Harris said. 'We're closing fast.'

Kennard stopped talking and Falcon pushed his drifting thoughts aside as they realized they were coming up to the shore and the river mouth. The maze of islets, shoals, sandbanks and shallows scattered around the delta would have made it a nightmare for any ordinary boat to navigate, and practically impossible except at daylight and high tide. However, the hovercraft simply whizzed over most of the obstacles, they had only to avoid the larger islets — and locate the main river channel.

Kennard had to concentrate now, but he was good at his job and obviously he had practised night penetrations of the rivers on the north coast. Harris advised another one degree correction and Kennard made the minimal adjustment to the rudders which were the moving fins of the double tailplane behind the propeller. He had slowed to 20 miles per hour and Falcon saw the dark blur of the coastline sweeping past on either side.

A low, solid mass loomed up abruptly. Kennard made deft movements of the controls and spray flew around the hovercraft as it made a sharp zigzag turn to waltz around what Falcon recognized seconds later as a small island.

Kennard straightened out their course and Falcon realized they were into the central channel of the river.

'There's sure to be a fleet of sampans moored off Batakan.' Kennard explained his cautious approach. 'We don't want to hit any of them.'

Falcon nodded his approval. Behind him the Gurkhas were calm and silent, like the two men at the controls they had been through this experience many times before. But for Gail it was something new. Falcon could sense her excitement as she sat tense beside him. When he looked at her she smiled, her lips slightly parted. At least she was enjoying it.

Dim yellow lights appeared ahead, scattered on either side of the river, and a moment later they were passing through the sprawl of untidy shacks and huts that was Batakan. The riverfront buildings were propped on stilts to raise them above the water, and many of them had canoes or sampans tied alongside.

There were large sampans, and one small Chinese junk, moored in midstream. Kennard weaved the hovercraft through them with practised ease, and apart from one sleepy yelp of alarm as they cast spray over a sampan there was nothing to indicate that their passage had been noted.

It was all faintly visible for a few seconds in the starlight, and then the town was behind them. With no submerged hull they made a minimum of waves; in fact at cruising and faster speeds the hovercraft would make no waves at all. The sound of their engine had been a swift, passing roar in the night, and it was doubtful if more than a handful of people had been fully awakened from their slumbers.

'A piece of cake,' Kennard said, looking back and smiling at the simplicity with which they had bypassed their first possible obstacle.

Once clear of the town he switched on their searchlight and the white beam made a dazzling lance into the darkness. The jungle showed up, dripping green upon black, and pressing close and threatening on either side. The surface of the river was a dark, villainous brown, swollen by the heavy rains in the interior, and swirling fast and swift beneath them.

A conventional boat would have made slow headway against the current, but again the hovercraft was unaffected.

The river made frequent twists and turns, curling lazily through the dense walls of jungle, but with the aid of the searchlight Kennard was able to increase his speed again. Harris had folded up the coastal chart, which was of no further use, but he still kept watch on the radar screen.

At any moment the river could make a hairpin bend, or divide around an island, or they could be endangered by an uprooted tree rushed downstream by the rains, so Kennard and Harris stayed constantly alert. They both knew all the possibilities and risks.

The others refrained from conversations, not wanting to distract the two men at the controls. The journey passed quickly and in silence, with mile after mile of the Kiamba passing like a ghost river in the night.

They were making good time, as fast as they could go in safety, but even so they were only about thirty miles upriver when the first pale shafts of pink began to break up the darkness of the eastern sky. Dawn had overtaken them too quickly, the transformation being even more instant than Falcon had expected, and it was daylight before they reached Surajong.

Now the jungle was revealed as a mass of huge clinging ferns, trailing vines, thorny undergrowth and foliage, all trailing down from the gigantic trees of the rainforest. It was sullen and hostile, and when the rare lagoon came into view to break the monotony of the river it was always gloomy and forbidding.

Only in one of the lagoons did they see a few poor village huts, and two drawn-up canoes on a mud-bar beach. There was no sign of the owners, who might have been peering terrified from within.

As the sun warmed up the air clouds of small flies and insects appeared hovering and buzzing, but otherwise there was no sign of life along the river. Falcon guessed there must be water snakes and crocodiles, and birds in the overhanging trees, but everything was passing in a blur.

Kennard had switched off the searchlight and now they were making an impressive 40 miles per hour on the airspeed indicator. Driving the SRN5 up the river was almost as easy as driving an automobile up a smooth highway, except for the more contorted and more frequent bends.

Surajong appeared ahead: a small town that was another cluster of propped up houses, a rickety bamboo and timber wharf, and a scattering of sampans and canoes cluttering the river. The crumbling prayer tower and faded dome of a small Moslem mosque were the only variation in the flat skyline.

'Drive through as fast as you can,' Falcon ordered Kennard. 'Ignore any signals to stop.'

Gail smiled. 'That will ruffle officialdom.'

'Too bad,' Falcon said seriously. 'But we can't afford any delays. The survivors at the crash site could be dying.'

Kennard eased his control stick forward, altering the pitch of the propeller blades to give more thrust. The hovercraft surged forward with increased speed and hurtled into Surajong.

The town was coming awake and there were startled faces along the waterfront. A sampan was putting out lazily from the right-hand bank and Kennard made a tight swerve to avoid it. They passed close enough to almost swamp the native craft and drew yelps and shrieks of rage and alarm.

More townspeople were running onto the wharf, most of them thin and dark-skinned in sarong or shorts, their eyes popping. Children shouted and pointed, some of them looking scared and others delighted.

Kennard swerved again to miss a canoe with a terrified fisherman who promptly toppled overboard, and a ragged cheer went up from those who welcomed the display.

A fat man in brown shirt and shorts ran along the wharf, waving his arms in agitation and blowing a whistle. He looked like a policeman and caused more howls of laughter when he tripped over the polished club-stick hanging from his belt which somehow became entangled between his legs.

Then they were through and Surajong was behind them. Ahead were the tangled jungle banks and the open river once more.

'That's it,' Kennard said. 'No more towns. The most we can expect to see now is the occasional fishing village. The chap in the brown shorts was probably the only government north of Batakan.'

He eased back on the stick and the hovercraft slowed to a more sedate 30 miles per hour.

'But we'll have to take a bit more care, because the river will narrow and it's all virtually unknown territory. As far as I know no boats go any higher than Surajong.'

However, the river still continued wide and deep, and Falcon was hopeful of getting all the way up to the crash site. They were all more relaxed in daylight and the Gurkhas were still laughing between themselves over the confusion they had left behind.

Falcon fished a pack of Benson & Hedges from the breast pocket of his shirt and offered them round. Kennard half turned to take one.

'Bend coming up, sir,' Harris warned.

Kennard returned his attention to the controls, the unlit cigarette still between the fingers of his left hand. Beyond the bend the river opened out suddenly into a maze of shallows and sandbanks, and he automatically eased off more speed as he followed the course of the main channel to where the river narrowed again into another bend which would bring it back on to the original course.

And it was on this next bend that they ran into the second ambush.

The machine guns had been set up one on either side of the river, and they erupted almost simultaneously into a murderous crossfire.

CHAPTER 5

The attack came as a complete surprise, and against any kind of conventional boat it would have had a devastating effect. Fortunately the hovercraft was armoured, designed for military use, and most of the gunfire simply ricocheted off her steel flanks in a deafening clatter of noise. Gail shrieked and Falcon pulled her down to the floor.

They were travelling close to the left-hand bank of the river and it was the left-hand side machine gun which drew blood. The front window crashed in under a burst of bullets and Tom Harris screamed with pain as he was flung sideways from his seat. He fell against Kennard's legs, hampering the young lieutenant as he struggled with the controls.

Falcon wriggled quickly forward and pushed the limp body back to its own side of the control deck.

Freed of the restraining weight Kennard was able to act. The machine guns were still ahead, they had opened fire a moment too soon. He had a choice of accelerating and going through, or using the wide sprawl of the river over the shallows to turn back. If he had been in mid-river he might have given her full boost and run the gauntlet, but he was coming up fast under the muzzle of the left bank machine gun. Harris had already been hit. More casualties were probable. And there was the serious risk of the rotor blades being smashed to leave them powerless and helpless before the enemy. Kennard made his decision and kicked hard on the rudder bar, swinging the hovercraft fast to the right, away from that merciless, close-range concentration of fire.

It was an instinctive more than a calculated reaction, and having made it he held it. The hovercraft spun in a tight turn which seemed as though it must end in a complete and disastrous somersault. But it was throwing up a high wave of spray as it twisted, and the water curtain was obscuring the aim of the machine gunners on both banks. More bullets hammered like steel hail off the armoured skirts but failed to find the weak spots of the windows.

For a split second the hovercraft was aimed straight at the right-hand bank. Kennard strained at the rudder bar with all his strength, fearing that he had miscalculated and that there wasn't going to be quite enough room to make the turn. If they rammed the bank and stuck fast they would still be at the mercy of the machine guns.

Desperately Kennard pulled back on the stick, slowing their speed but still maintaining the tight turn. Another window caved in behind him but no scream echoed the crash of breaking glass. Then the hovercraft's bow was brushing the overhanging ferns and foliage of the jungle bank. She completed the turn with thorns and branches flailing the length of her hull and sliced leaves and greenery flying from the blurred circle of the propeller.

Kennard rammed the stick forward again and at full speed raced back downstream, away from the ambush.

Falcon had eased Harris back down the centre aisle between the passenger seats. The sergeant's face was white and the upper part of his left arm was blood-soaked.

'Give me some room, Mark.'

He looked up and saw Gail on her hands and knees beside him. She was dragging out her medical bag from beneath the seat and he squeezed over to let her examine Harris.

Quickly she snipped away the torn shirtsleeve with her scissors. Harris was conscious and gritting his teeth.

'Easy, Tom,' she told him gently. 'Try and relax now.'

Falcon straightened up his head and shoulders to check out the rest of the damage. The Gurkhas all appeared to be in one piece, crouching low, submachine guns unslung, and all looking more indignant and frustrated than anything else. Bahadur Rama had his head and shoulders out of the smashed mid-section window, but he couldn't fire back upriver without risking damage to the propeller. His taut little body bristled with impotent anger.

A few seconds later the river made another bend. The scene of the ambush was screened off by the jungle, out of sight and out of range.

Falcon called to one of the Gurkhas and let him take over the job of supporting Harris while Gail worked. Then he stood up and went forward. Kennard glanced at him, tight-lipped.

'Tom will be okay,' Falcon assured him. 'Two bullets passed through the upper left arm. Messy and painful, but he'll survive.'

'The bastards,' Kennard swore. 'Who the hell—?'

'I don't know,' Falcon said. 'But we'll find out. Pull over to the bank, Pete, and stop.'

Kennard obeyed, pulling back on the stick to slow the hovercraft, and then holding her with just enough reverse thrust to maintain a standstill position against the push of the current.

'We could try again,' Kennard said grimly. 'This time we know what to expect so I'll take her through the middle at top speed. With everybody flat on the floor we should be able to avoid any more casualties. The big problem is we take a fifty-fifty risk with the prop blades. If they get smashed—'

Falcon shook his head. 'The people on that plane need better than a fifty per cent chance. And remember we have to come back the same way. Two runs through that ambush means overall only a twenty-five per cent chance of mission success.'

'Then how?'

Falcon said simply. 'We clear those machine guns out of the way.'

He turned. 'Sergeant Rama!'

'Yes, sah!' Bahadur Rama withdrew his head and shoulders into the hovercraft and came promptly forward.

'Disembark your men on the left-hand bank. I want you to move forward and take that machine gun post. Kill the gunners, if you have to, whoever they are, and make sure you destroy the gun. They think we've turned tail and fled, so it may be easy. But don't count on it.'

'Yes, sah!' The Gurkha sergeant beamed fiercely and joyously as he turned to relay their orders to his men.

'What about the other gun? The one on the right bank?' Kennard ask slowly.

'I'll deal with that one,' Falcon answered calmly. He reached for the Sterling submachine gun that was strapped behind the navigator's seat. 'Tom won't be able to use this, so I guess he won't mind if I borrow it.'

Gail looked up from the task of fixing a wound dressing to Harris's arm. 'Alone?' she queried, and her face was worried.

'It's okay.' Falcon smiled without humour. 'I have had previous experience in these jungles.'

'Of course, all those years with S.A.S.' She remembered the conversation with Norville, but her face remained doubtful.

'There's no need to go alone.' Kennard pulled his own weapon from behind his seat, and rammed home a full magazine with an angry movement. 'I'm coming with you.'

Falcon said gently. 'Someone has to guard the hovercraft.'

Kennard hesitated, but his face was set. 'Detail a couple of the Gurkhas.'

Falcon frowned slightly, staring at Kennard. The young lieutenant held the stare.

Falcon knew he could order Kennard to stay behind. He was in command of this mission and Kennard knew it. But Kennard and Harris were friends, and if he forced Kennard to remain behind then Kennard would inevitably lose face with the watching Gurkhas.

Falcon preferred to go alone. He would be faster and more certain. Kennard had no actual combat experience and could be a liability. But Kennard had all the right potential, and to be fair he had to be given his chance.

Falcon relented and nodded. 'Okay, Pete, you come with me, but stay close off my left flank.'

He turned to give final instructions to Bahadur Rama.

'Leave two men here, sergeant. Give Lieutenant Kennard and myself five minutes start and then move your men up. When you hear gunfire on the right bank it will distract the enemy on your side. That's your signal to move in and mop up.'

'Yes, sah!' The Gurkha sergeant saluted, spoke quickly to his men in Nepalese, and then led four of them ashore.

The two who remained looked glum, but as for the others, Falcon had never seen men go off to battle so happily.

Kennard steered the SRN5 across the river and Falcon threw out the anchor to hold her against the right bank. Kennard switched off the engine and when the sound faded there was nothing left except the fast, rushing gurgle of the passing current.

They helped Harris into a more comfortable sitting position on one of the passenger seats. Gail had dressed his wounds, made the arm comfortable in a sling, and given him a painkilling injection.

'How are you feeling?' Kennard asked.

'Okay.' Harris lied. He was pale and shaken. 'Go get 'em, sir.'

Falcon smiled. 'Don't go ashore,' he warned Gail. 'And keep your heads down. This won't take long.'

Gail nodded. She was bearing up well, fully in command of herself, but not quite cheerful enough to return the smile.

Kennard produced two long-bladed parang knives in scabbards and passed one to Falcon. They needed the heavy jungle knives to cut their way ashore, for the thick green foliage formed an almost impenetrable wall.

When they had hacked a passage a few yards deep they looked back. The Gurkhas had vanished on the far bank, having used their kukris to cut their way into the jungle.

Kennard was already dripping sweat in the steamy heat.

'Hell,' he said. 'We're about a mile downstream from those machine guns. If we've got to cut a path all the way back it will take us hours.'

'I don't think we'll have to,' Falcon comforted him. 'I didn't see any boats at the ambush site, so whoever set it up they must have used jungle paths following the river up from Surajong. My guess is we'll strike into a path before we get much further.'

They attacked the wall of ferns and creeper again, and within three minutes Falcon was proved right. They forced their way on to a narrow path that had been well trodden by native feet.

They turned north and found they were able to move swiftly, following the course of the river upstream. Falcon hoped that the Gurkhas had been as lucky on the other side.

For ten minutes they hurried forward. Falcon was counting the bends in the river and calculating the distance, thankful for those early days in Borneo that had sharpened his instincts and his judgement. He had sheathed the parang once they had found the path, and now the submachine gun was a comfortable and familiar weight in his hands. All his senses were primed and alert. He was combat ready and feeling sharp.

Where the river made its wide loop the land formed a large, shallow basin of bared rock strata and poor soil. The rainforest had no hold here, it was a patch of choked ravines and small trees. Orchids made splashes of brilliant colour among the thorn bushes.

The machine gun had been mounted on its tripod on a small knoll, and the undergrowth cut back with parangs to give it a clear field of fire over the river.

Five men were grouped around it. One man was braced behind the gun, another squatted beside it with the ammunition belt held loosely ready to feed through his hands. The other three men held Kalashnikov, AK-47 combat rifles.

All were staring downriver. Waiting. Hoping the hovercraft would come back.

The sunlight glinted off the deeper channels between the sandbars. Flies buzzed. Otherwise there was stillness.

After ten minutes they began to grin at each other, hiding their disappointment because the hovercraft had not come back. At least they had chased it away. That in itself was a victory.

They began to relax.

Falcon had cautioned Kennard to silence before they emerged from the forest, explaining carefully the hand signals he would use. The path led them directly to the machine gun, and a glimpse of the river told them they must be very near.

Falcon paused, tapped Kennard on the shoulder, pointed to their left, and made the sign for keeping low.

Kennard nodded. His face was tense and wet with perspiration, but the sun felt hot enough to melt rock. His grip on the Sterling was steady enough and he moved purposefully off the path to the left.

Falcon moved off to the right. They continued forward and immediately heard voices just ahead.

Falcon smiled, but did not get overconfident. He eased forward another step, and then another. He could see the raised knoll with the machine gun and the five men through the tangle of boulders and bushes and he froze.

He indicated silently to Kennard to do the same.

They waited.

Falcon tested the air with his senses. After a full minute the reading was still five. There was no other voice or movement.

He moved forward and called sharply.

'Throw down your weapons.'

The five men whirled. Their reaction times varied and even if they understood the command none of them obeyed it. The man behind the machine gun swung round with it, his finger tightening on the trigger. The others fumbled with the combat rifles.

They were all too slow. Falcon had moved lightning fast, stepping to the right where he had already checked there was nothing to trip him up, moving into a half crouch and firing his submachine gun from the hip.

The man at the heavy machine gun was blasted backward, with bright poppies of blood flowering across his chest. The machine gun sagged back on its tripod and the long barrel kicked up to fire a blind burst at the sky.

The three men with the combat rifles were scattering, answering Falcon's fire. Falcon zapped the nearest one with a burst, disintegrating his head in a blood and bone fountain.

Falcon was still moving, too fast for the combat rifles to catch up with him. He shot number two with a burst into the stomach and a burst from Kennard killed number three.

But Kennard had fired from a standing position. He was tense and rigid, not moving.

The last man, the man who had squatted ready to ensure the free movement of the belt feed, had sprawled flat on the grass. Quickly he had wriggled his rifle from his shoulder and aimed. He fired at the easier target.

Falcon was sprinting forward from the right, sweeping the prone man with bullets, rolling the abruptly bloodied corpse across the short slope to the river.

But the damage had been done. Kennard was spun round, a hot, bleeding groove burned across his left temple. He pitched headlong, facing back the way they had come.

Falcon swore. He quickly checked out the five dead men, making sure they were as lifeless as they appeared to be. In Aden and Oman he had seen supposedly dead rebel tribesmen rise up again to shoot their enemies in the back.

This time there was nothing to worry about. Falcon ran back to Kennard.

The young British officer lay very still and for a moment Falcon feared the worst. Quickly but gently he turned the body over and examined the wound, then he breathed a sigh of relief.

Kennard was unconscious but he had only been creased. With luck he would wake with nothing worse than a duelling scar and a gigantic headache.

Deftly Falcon strapped a wound dressing around Kennard's head. While he worked he heard the sharp crackle of automatic fire from the far side of the river and paused to listen. The sound of the British Sterlings was dominant over the quickly silenced chatter of the Kalashnikovs.

A shriek sounded, shrill and fearful, echoing across the shallows and the sandbars. Somehow Falcon knew that even if wounded or dying the Gurkhas would not be the type to scream. He remembered the wicked kukris and smiled grimly.

Precisely on cue, Sergeant Bahadur Rama was mopping up.

CHAPTER 6

It was oven-hot inside the hovercraft. The motionless vehicle absorbed the fierce heat of the sun and held it until Gail felt as though she was trapped inside a Turkish bath. Her shirt was glued to her flesh, sticky and uncomfortable, and if the two Gurkha soldiers had not been there she would have stripped to her bra.

Harris was also sweating profusely, and all she could do for him was to give him sips of water and endeavour to wipe him dry.

For a while she stared at the river, watching the swirling tracks of the water snakes. Every river in Borneo was full of them, and most of them were poisonous. Somewhere close by there would be crocodiles, ugly and watchful, laying up in the shade. Gail had seen them often enough in Sarawak. She shivered at the thought. No matter how hot it became, this was no place for a bathe.

The waiting frayed at her nerves.

She wondered what the hell was she doing here. She was a doctor, top of her class, fully qualified. She could have worked in any one of a hundred fully equipped, up-to-date, beautifully air-conditioned hospitals in the United States! Instead she had come to work in North Borneo with a bottle of aspirins and a pair of blunt scissors. And now this! How had she ever volunteered for this?

But she hadn't volunteered. Norville had sent a launch upriver from Kuching to fetch her because she was the only white doctor within a thousand miles. And because there were people in trouble she had jumped on board. She hadn't even thought to argue.

She smiled to herself and wiped sweat from her face with the back of her hand. Good old Gail! Never say no. Perhaps she should try the same policy with men. Life might be more fun, and less sweat and hard bloody work.

Men, her thoughts drifted in the heat. Mark Falcon! Now there was a real man. She found him both fascinating and frightening. She couldn't help but notice that he was a superb example of the male body. All those hard, rangy muscles and not an ounce of surplus fat. If all men kept their bodies in that kind of shape there would be less work for doctors, and, she smiled again, more fun for women.

There was a positive radiance of male electricity from Falcon that made her tingle when she was close to him. No other man had ever affected her like this, and she had the feeling he was interested in her. Maybe later they should get together. The very thought made her tingle too.

Yes, Mark Falcon was a very special man, but there was another side to him that made her feel cold. The ice-cool, commanding side of his nature that was immediately revealed in a crisis. Falcon had killed three men in Kuching and he had not been troubled. Now he was somewhere in the jungle preparing to kill more men.

Gail felt that she should be anxious for Falcon. After all, her own hope of getting safely back to civilization was probably dependent upon his safe return. But she wasn't worried.

Instead she felt a fleeting pity for the men who had staged the ambush. How could they know they had brought down upon themselves such a grim angel of retribution.

Faintly from upriver she heard the first sharp exchange of gunfire. A few minutes later it was repeated and then there was silence again except for the gurgle of the river and the buzz of the flies. The heat and the waiting continued.

Twenty minutes passed before the two Gurkhas abruptly became alert, levelling their weapons and staring at the cut path into the jungle. Gail stared with them and another sixty seconds passed before she heard the swish of foliage. The sounds came closer, making no attempt at silence, and then Falcon appeared with Kennard draped over his shoulders.

The two soldiers hurried to help lift the injured man on board, and Gail stared shocked at the red-stained head bandage. Somehow she had known that Falcon would return unscathed. But she had forgotten about Kennard.

'It's okay,' Falcon said. 'It's only a bullet crease.'

He was breathing deeply and his shirt was stained in huge patches of sweat, but otherwise it was difficult to believe that he had just carried a one-hundred-and-forty pound deadweight through a mile of jungle heat.

They got the unconscious Kennard into the passenger seat behind Harris and Gail checked him over. The head dressing had been correctly applied and there was little more she could do except apply another layer of bandages to cover the bloodstain.

'They both need hospitalization,' she told Falcon when she had finished. 'In this climate wounds can soon become infected.'

'I know,' Falcon said calmly. 'But first we have to pick up a planeload of passengers.'

She stared at him, eyes flashing. 'Peter is going to be very sick and groggy when he wakes up. He'll have to drive us back down the river, but he certainly isn't going to be fit enough to carry on.'

'It's okay,' Falcon said again. 'I have a pilot's licence. I can fly light aircraft and helicopters, and pilot small boats. Piloting the SRN5 is a combination of both skills, but I have been watching Peter and I understand his controls. I can handle it.'

Gail realized that somehow she should have known. He was the kind of man who would be able to handle almost anything.

Falcon started up the hovercraft, turned it round to face back upstream, and moved it over to the opposite bank to pick up the remaining Gurkhas. A few minutes later Bahadur Rama and his four companions appeared and filed on board. They were all unscathed, all full of smiles and well pleased with themselves.

Falcon had noted that both the Gurkha sergeant and Corporal Ganju had drawn their kukris to cut a path through the undergrowth when they had left the hovercraft. Now the weapons were sheathed but there was no sign of a small, ritual incision on the fingers of either man. The obligatory blood the kukris had tasted had been the blood of their enemies.

Bahadur Rama made his report as Falcon piloted the hovercraft upstream. Four men of the unknown enemy lay dead on the left bank. Their weapons had been thrown into the river, the machine gun after Bahadur Rama had taken the double precaution of bending the barrel between two boulders.

Falcon had done the same with the machine gun on his side.

They came on to the wide loop of the river over the shallows and skimmed over the ambush area without hindrance. Gail was silent as she stared at each bank in turn, trying to find some sign of death and bloodshed, but there was nothing. Tangles of rocks, bushes, jungle ferns and flowers hid whatever had happened.

She saw one glimpse of bright red through the grey and green, but it might have been only an orchid.

The river plunged into the rainforest again and continued as before. The hovercraft raced on beneath the dark green walls of overhanging vines and branches.

'Who were they?' Gail asked at last. 'The people who attacked us?'

She had taken the navigator's seat and Falcon glanced at her sombre face and shrugged briefly before returning his gaze to the river.

'I don't know. I'd say they were Indonesians. Most of them young — in their twenties. No uniforms, so unlikely to have been Indonesian government troops. Plus their weapons were all of Soviet origin. Most of them carried a Kalashnikov AK-47. The machine guns were both Dectyaryovs.'

He paused then added. 'If I had to typecast them I'd say they came from the same mould as the gang that tried to stop me in Kuching. Left-wing students, trained and indoctrinated in Libya, Syria, or the Soviet Union.'

'But why? I mean why are they here — on this godforsaken river up the backside of nowhere?'

'A good question,' Falcon acknowledged. 'I wish I knew the answer. One thing is sure. The ambush party could only have come from Surajong, so it would seem that Surajong is not the forgotten little backwater it is supposed to be.'

'But it just doesn't make sense. Why should anyone want to stop us? And how could they know we were coming?'

'We could have been identified as we passed through Batakan. A radio call would have given enough warning for the ambush to be set up behind Surajong.'

'But I don't see why. We're on a mercy mission!'

'So we are. But international terrorism is sprouting everywhere. And most terrorists are merciless. Anybody's blood will do for the cause.'

'Terrorists.' She was bewildered. 'On a river in Borneo!'

He smiled wryly. 'I'm only guessing. And I don't know what else to guess at. Maybe we'll find out before the job is through — or when we get back to Kuching. I just might go looking for Norville's friend, the Mongolian Weasel, and wring out a few answers.

'In the meantime we keep our sights on one target. To find that plane. That's our Number One priority.'

The hours and the miles flowed by. The hot air rushed in through the broken windows but at least it was better than when the hovercraft had been stationary. Falcon had quickly got the feel of the controls and while the river flowed broad and deep he was able to maintain a steady cruising speed.

Slowly the river narrowed, with the jungle pressing closer like some palpitating, green and gloomy, living thing. They had left behind the long, lazy loops near sea level, and the Kiamba twisted and turned more erratically as the hovercraft pushed ever deeper into the interior and ever higher up toward the central ranges.

With every mile Falcon was forced to ease back on the stick and proceed with more caution.

The sun became a white blaze overhead, but the humidity showed no sign of drying out.

As the riverbanks squeezed the river they became more rocky and the hovercraft encountered the first stretch of rapids. The river foamed white around knuckles of brown stone, and its spate built up into a rushing roar that was louder than the whir of the propeller and the note of the engine.

Kennard was still unconscious but Tom Harris leaned forward painfully.

'Back on the stick, sir,' he advised Falcon. 'But maintain full engine power for maximum lift. She'll clear obstacles up to about three feet. Anything over that you'll have to go round.'

'Thanks, Tom,' Falcon smiled. 'I'll try to keep her in one piece.'

He moved the hovercraft forward slowly, weaving from side to side to bypass the larger boulders protruding above the turbulent waters. Gail sat tight-lipped and silent behind him. Once he brushed the armoured skirt of the hovercraft lightly against the rock wall and from behind him he heard Tom Harris wince.

After two hundred yards the strip of violent white water ended. The river flowed dark green between palms, giant jungle ferns and tangles of lush plants and foliage. A few yards back the rainforest began again, with towering trees making great domes of branches and trailing vines a hundred feet high.

Falcon eased the stick forward and increased their speed, hurrying upstream as fast as he dared.

Sixty seconds later the sky went black. The rain fell. It was not just a storm but a full-blooded tropical deluge. The falling water made a blinding curtain, forcing Falcon to slow again to a crawl. Like the thunder of a waterfall the rain poured over the SRN5, streaming over the windows and bursting inside where the windows had been broken.

Falcon cursed. They could ill afford the delay. At the same time it was a sign that they were approaching their target area, the high interior where the storms were still raging around the mountains.

The noise of the storm was deafening, and it sounded as though the forest was being ripped to pieces. Leaves were shredded, branches were torn down, and whole trees crashed into the undergrowth.

Falcon pulled close against the bank, stopped the hovercraft and held her there against the push of the current. The whipping foliage drummed a hellish tattoo along the windows but he ignored it.

Gail put her hands over her ears and gave him a questioning glance. However, before she could put the question into words the wisdom of the move became obvious. A massive tree branch came hurtling down the midstream current, its broken, jagged, white-toothed end missing them by inches as it was swirled past.

If Falcon had not anticipated the danger it would have smashed into them in head-on collision, and more broken branches and uprooted trees followed it downstream as the storm continued.

After thirty minutes, as suddenly as it had begun, the downpour stopped. The sky brightened as though some giant hand had flipped back a black blanket and the sun blazed through. The river and the dripping, mutilated jungle steamed.

Falcon put the hovercraft into motion again, keeping close to the left-hand bank now in case there was any more storm debris to be swept down from the upper reaches.

Kennard had at last recovered consciousness and Gail went back to check over both her patients.

They passed two more stretches of broken rapids, and then came to a narrow gorge where the river boiled in strangled white fury. Its roar was the most fearsome sound yet, and when she saw the booming explosions of spray Gail bit her lip and looked scared.

Falcon frowned. He calculated that they were about seventy miles upriver and it wasn't quite far enough. This was one of the most difficult countries in the world to travel on foot, and so they had to make the maximum advantage of the river to get as close as possible to the crash site. Every mile they made would save them hours of gruelling foot-slogging.

He had slowed almost to a stop and his jaw was set tight as he eased the SRN5 slowly forward into the maelstrom of the gorge. He could sense the tension in his companions but no one spoke.

Almost immediately the hovercraft became difficult to control. The air cushion kept it above the rushing water, but the air cushion itself was distorted by the violent upheavals of the river surface. Spray burst in great dazzling sheets from the surrounding rocks and the hovercraft twisted and lurched under the impact.

A boat would have perished in the first few seconds, but yard by yard Falcon pushed the bucking hovercraft up through the narrow defile. The walls rose steeper and tightened on either side, the jutting ribs of spray-washed black rock glinting evilly as they pushed toward midstream. The river had the sound of an express train thundering through a tunnel, and the exploding sunlight and water patterns of the bursting spume were both terrifying and beautiful.

A large rock in midstream would have forced them back, and an encounter with any large obstacle of storm debris could have spelled disaster. But fortunately they met neither. At the narrowest turn of the gorge they had only a few feet on either side to manoeuvre, but here the rock walls were worn smooth.

The hovercraft climbed up cautiously through the gorge and after five or six nerve-wracking minutes gained the comparatively clear water beyond. Behind him Falcon heard his companions begin breathing again.

They made a few more easy miles before the river turned another of its many bends, and opened out into a wide, jungle-flanked lagoon. There was more white water on the far side where the river entered, but this time the obstacle was impassable.

The river was pouring down over a thirty foot sheer drop, and not even the hovercraft could climb a waterfall.

Falcon pulled over to the left-hand side of the lagoon and nosed up on to a small, black mud beach. There he raised the skirt, cut the engine, and allowed the SRN5 to settle gently to rest.

'We've arrived,' he announced. For the river would take them no further.

This was their first real stop, and Falcon took the opportunity to make radio contact with *Scotsman*. The destroyer was within their range as she waited off the river mouth, and after five minutes of fine-tuning the set he received an answer.

He gave their status report and asked for a weather forecast. The change was small. The sky was clear overhead which would be some help, but further north the mountains and the whole of Sarawak were still taking a non-stop battering from the torrential rains.

An air search from Kuching was still impossible. For any who had survived on the crashed plane the SRN5 expedition was still their only hope.

Falcon signed off and pulled out his map. He stared down at the neat cross in red ink. If the map was correct, and his own estimate of the distance they had travelled, and if the pilot had given an accurate fix of his position, then the plane must be only a few miles away on the left bank.

If they were all lucky it might be found quickly.

If they were lucky.

In this kind of jungle they could pass within twenty yards of a lost city and never know it was there.

It had been a long morning and while Falcon still worked the rest of the party had made their way ashore to relieve themselves. Gail was the first to come back into the hovercraft and her gaze took quick note of the empty seats.

'Mark, where's Peter?'

Falcon looked up. 'I would imagine on the same errand as you.'

'But he left before me. He's been gone a good ten minutes. He shouldn't really be alone in the sun with that head wound.'

Falcon nodded agreement. She was right and he should have realized it. Being busy was no excuse. He got up and hurried down the door ramp to the beach.

The Gurkhas were boiling up water on a primus stove to make tea. Harris sat on a log watching them. Falcon rapped swift orders and the Gurkhas spread out quickly to find Kennard.

The search ended when Bahadur Rama called Falcon to join him five minutes later. A small stream filtered down through the jungle into the lagoon. The Gurkha sergeant crouched beside it.

Floating face down in the stream was Peter Kennard, and fresh blood was still seeping from a gaping and cruelly hacked wound in the back of his neck.

CHAPTER 7

Kennard was dead.

The fact hit them like a hammer blow, chilling their blood and numbing their senses. There had been nothing to warn them. No outcry of alarm. No sound of a scuffle. Nothing but the wet dripping of the trees, the buzz of insects, and the occasional flutter of butterflies and bright bird's wings across the lagoon.

And yet Kennard was dead. He had walked away from the hovercraft to unzip his fly and someone had cut him down, silently, and with cold-blooded efficiency.

With help from Bahadur Rama, Falcon retrieved the sprawled body from the stream. The head was lolling, half severed by the force of the killing blow.

The Gurkhas had come running. They stared in disbelief, and then at a sign from Bahadur Rama they unslung their weapons and formed a circle, facing outward, searching the jungle gloom for the unseen enemy.

Gail pushed herself between two of the grim-faced little Nepalese. She saw what had happened and retched, turning quickly away.

Tom Harris followed her more slowly. He too looked totally shocked, his face draining as white as the sling supporting his injured arm.

'Jesus Christ,' he groaned. 'Oh, sweet, suffering Jesus Christ!'

Falcon moved to block Gail's view and lead her away. She resisted the attempt, breathing deeply a couple of times, and then pushing his hand from her shoulder.

'It's okay, Mark. I've seen worse from automobile accidents. It's just that it was so unexpected. And it's worse when it's someone you know.'

She breathed deeply again, and then steeled herself to turn and examine Kennard. She knelt briefly beside the body.

'He must have died instantly,' she decided. She looked up and her voice was strained. 'With his head swimming from that first bullet wound he probably never knew what hit him. He was killed with some kind of heavy knife, a native parang, or—' Her voice faltered as she glanced toward the nearest Gurkha. 'Or a kukri.'

It took a moment for her meaning to sink in. Then Bahadur Rama drew himself stiffly to attention. His face was pained and his whole body trembled with anger and indignation.

'No, sah!' He told Falcon. 'This was not done by any of my men. No, sah. No, sah! Never!'

Falcon stared into the fierce, unflinching eyes and believed him. But it left the big question unanswered. Kennard had been murdered. But by whom?

'Get him back to the hovercraft,' he ordered grimly. 'We can't leave him here for crocodile meat. Then spread your men out in pairs to look for any sign of who did this.

'Gail and Tom, back into the hovercraft. From now on nobody moves out of my sight alone.'

The search drew a blank. Except for a couple of long abandoned native huts and some overgrown footpaths there was no sign that anyone but themselves had ever been near the lagoon. The natives who had once lived here had either died or moved on.

This was Dayak country. The expanding Malays, Javanese, Arabs and Chinese who occupied the coastal settlement towns would never have pushed this far upriver. The huts had belonged to the primitive, indigenous headhunters.

But the Dayaks were supposed to be cured of their ancient custom of collecting heads. They had taken the trophies for revenge, ritual and prestige, but the old Dutch colonialists were supposed to have stamped all those old practices out.

Well, perhaps the Dutch hadn't been as successful as they believed.

Perhaps a stray headhunter had returned.

And perhaps not.

The only other answer was to believe that Kennard had been killed by one of their own party. The bristling Bahadur Rama? Skinny Corporal Ganju? One of the soldiers — or all of them together in some treacherous conspiracy?

He didn't think so.

Who then? Tom Harris carried a heavy army sheath knife at his hip, and considering Kennard's weakened state, Harris could have used the knife with one hand?

Or perhaps Gail? She had taken one of the parangs when she went to pee, presumably to cut her way through the undergrowth, or to protect herself from the odd snake or lizard. Perhaps she had cut down Kennard instead?

It was crazy. Falcon realized that his brain was whirling in the heat. He would be suspecting himself next — and perhaps some of the others already did.

None of them had any motive.

But with or without a motive Kennard remained undeniably dead.

One of their own party, or a passing stranger in a primitive wilderness where there were no passing strangers. There was nowhere else to look for the murderer.

When all the searching had been done, both mentally and physically, the priority job still remained. They still had to find the crashed plane.

They were all angry, suspicious of each other, and in Gail's case more than a little afraid. Falcon had to hold them together. The mystery of Kennard's death was unsolved, a black, sinister shadow hanging over them all. Their mission carried the mark of Cain, the taint of possible treachery from within, but they had to go on.

Falcon promised himself that he would find the answer, and someone would pay for the brutal lulling of Peter Kennard, but right now there was no time to waste.

He faced them all on the mud beach beside the hovercraft.

'I'll take Sergeant Rama and four of the Gurkhas,' he told them grimly. 'Gail, you'll have to come with us. We'll need you when we find the plane.'

Gail nodded. Her face was pale but her medical bag was packed and ready. Falcon looked to Harris.

'Tom, you'll have to stay behind. I'm sorry, but with that arm you won't stand up to a rough trek through the jungle. Besides, in the circumstances I dare not leave the hovercraft unguarded. I'll leave two of the Gurkhas with you.'

Harris nodded understanding. His face was bleak and he had nothing to say. He had reclaimed his submachine gun, holding it in his right hand with the strap over his sound shoulder, and obviously he had no intention of letting it go.

Falcon knew he was taking a calculated risk in splitting his party. By leaving Harris with two of the Nepalese he could be condemning the British sergeant to death if the Gurkhas were disloyal. On the other hand, if Harris was the traitor he could lose two Gurkhas.

But there was no real choice.

'Stay on board the hovercraft,' he advised Harris.

'Yes, sir.' Harris let the words grate through his teeth. His arm still gave him pain and he was not happy. Perhaps he had worked out all the possibilities too.

Bahadur Rama detailed the two Gurkhas who were to stay behind. Falcon led the rest of them into the jungle. He was carrying a parang again — and Kennard's Sterling. This time it was the young lieutenant who would have no need for a weapon.

During the search around the lagoon Falcon had climbed above the waterfall where the river entered. He had gained as much height as he could, but it had not been enough for him to see over the tops of the surrounding trees. However, he knew that was his only hope of finding the crashed plane. He had to first find a ridge or a hill where he could get above the dense jungle blanket and use his binoculars. If there was no high ground it could prove to be a long and probably hopeless task.

Of the three footpaths the Gurkhas had discovered, two followed the river, upstream and downstream. The third led off along the course of the little side stream where Kennard's body had been found. Water flowed downhill, so Falcon reasoned that his best chance of finding a viewpoint would be to follow the stream toward its source. There was also the thought that it might be leading them toward Kennard's killer. If so, that would be a bonus.

The path had not been used for some time, the jungle was reclaiming it. In places Falcon had to chop down the fast-sprouting foliage with the parang, but it was the only path there was. It wound a tortuous route beside the stream, but to try and force a new path in any sort of direct line through the virgin jungle would have taken twice as long.

Paths did not exist for nothing. There had to be something at the end of it. Probably more native huts. Perhaps disease had forced them back from the river? Perhaps there were headhunters at the end of the path, or perhaps they had all died anyway. It was all conjecture, but Falcon moved warily.

There was a prickling sensation between his shoulder blades. Gail was immediately behind him, and then Bahadur Rama and the Gurkhas. Perhaps the real danger was there. He was a sitting duck at the head of the column.

He hesitated, then felt the insect slip lower inside his shirt and realized what it was. He reached back awkwardly to slap at it. In the jungle insects, twigs and pollen and other irritations, were always falling from the trees.

He moved on. If the Gurkhas, as a group, were not loyal, then he was a dead man anyway. It had to be one, or two of them, or none at all. The whole squad had enough firepower to finish himself, Gail and Harris, without any need for stealth and cunning.

The sweat began to ooze out of him. It was hot, hard work, even though the canopy of trees shut out the sunlight overhead. Birds flew in the high branches, but on the forest floor all was gloomy with the rich smell of rot and mould. Mosquitoes, moths and beetles were the only things that moved, although he knew that wild pig, leopard and other animals roamed at will. Borneo was the third largest island on earth, and possessed most of the still relatively unexplored jungle that was left.

Behind him he could hear Gail stumbling and breathing heavily as she struggled to maintain the pace. Behind her the

Gurkhas made very little noise. They had been trained for jungle work.

For two hours they made steady progress, then the terrain began to slope upward. It was extra toil on the aching leg muscles, but Falcon's hopes lifted. He pushed on for another half mile, with the path climbing up beside the stream all the time. Then he called a brief halt.

They rested, drinking sparingly from water bottles and eating a few bars of emergency ration chocolate. The Gurkhas looked unruffled, and one of them was carrying Gail's shoulder bag. Gail looked weary.

'You okay?' Falcon asked.

She smiled faintly. 'I think I've got blisters on my heels, and leeches inside my shirt. Otherwise, ask me when I get my second wind.'

Falcon smiled back. 'Take your shirt off,' he ordered.

She stared at him, then obeyed. The Gurkhas politely looked the other way while Falcon carefully removed the leeches from her skin, touching their blood-bloated bodies with the hot end of a lighted cigarette until they dropped off. If they were pulled off the heads would stay inside the flesh and fester.

Gail put her shirt back on and performed the same service for the rest of them. Between them they had collected over a score of the blood-sucking little creatures.

They moved on again. This time Falcon handed over the parang and let one of the Gurkhas take the lead. The little soldier set a good pace, and Falcon found himself helping Gail more and more often as the steepness of the path increased.

Finally, after another hour of hard, uphill slogging, they broke out of the rainforest and found themselves on the steep upper slope of a spinal ridge that was covered in long, tough grass, thorn bushes and ferns. Bare bones of moss-covered rock pushed through the earth, and the sunlight was suddenly blinding from the blue-white glare of the sky.

They paused again, taking in their new surroundings, and a few more sips of their precious water.

The path they had been following veered away from the stream and continued in a diagonal line to the top of the ridge. Falcon saw it with satisfaction. It meant there was a chance.

He led on quickly to the top of the ridge and there made a complete three-hundred-and-sixty-degree scan with his binoculars. On all sides the treetops washed against the island ridge in dark green waves, with no sign of a break except the groove line to the east which marked the course of the Kiamba. There was nothing to show where a plane might have gone down. No thread of smoke from a signal fire.

Falcon made the scan again, slowly this time, searching until his eyes ached in the fierce glare. Still there was nothing but the vast, still sea of jungle green.

Bahadur Rama stood beside him. The others squatted or sat where they could make themselves comfortable. Gail had flopped out almost exhausted.

Falcon handed the binoculars to the Gurkha sergeant, hoping the other man might have keener eyes. Bahadur Rama made the same sweeping search, but after five minutes shook his head regretfully.

Falcon had brought along the signal pistol that was part of the emergency equipment on the hovercraft. He fitted a cartridge and fired it into the air. Red and green star shells burst briefly, high over the jungle.

He fired three more cartridges, one in each direction. After each shot they watched and waited. The crashed plane should have had a similar flare pistol on board. If there were survivors they should be able to fire an answer.

But there was nothing.

Bahadur Rama called up his corporal. 'Best eyes in Nepal,' he explained proudly, and hopefully, as he handed Ganju the glasses.

For ten minutes the thin little man stood rigid with the binoculars pressed to his eyes. He stood splay-legged, moving his feet inch by inch as he examined the treetops from east to west. He was halfway round the circle when he stopped, facing north-west. Then he lowered the glasses and grinned at Bahadur Rama. He pointed and spoke quickly in Nepalese.

The sergeant looked again, beamed, and handed the glasses back to Falcon.

'He is right, sah. Over there! Perhaps two miles. A place where the top branches of the trees are broken.'

Falcon looked. At first he saw nothing. Then he distinguished a break in the rolling flow of green. It was so poorly defined he wasn't sure whether his eyes were playing tricks in the heat haze. But it could be a clearing — or a hole in the jungle canopy where the plane had gone down.

He lowered the glasses and looked at Ganju. The corporal grinned more widely, showing broken white teeth. He was happy and confident.

And there was nothing else to aim for.

'Okay,' Falcon decided. He checked the compass course. 'Let's cut our way over there.'

They picked up their weapons and packs. Bahadur Rama took the parang, and together he and Falcon led the way down the north-west slope of the ridge.

CHAPTER 8

It took them another three hours of hard, physical effort to cut a direct line through the virgin jungle. If they had detoured to find the route of least resistance they might have missed their target altogether, so the only way was to follow the precise compass direction which Falcon had carefully noted before they began their forced advance. The Gurkhas took the lead in turn, hacking a path with vigorous, slashing strokes of the parang. The sun was high overhead and five minutes at a time was enough for that kind of work in the murderous, strength-sapping heat. Falcon and Bahadur Rama kept the column rotating and took their own turn with the parang when it came.

Gail was the only one who did no work, maintaining her place in the middle of the line, walking slowly, and feeling as though she was caught up in some unreal and feverish bad dream. Her limbs felt heavy as lead, her shirt was wet with sweat, her hair was bedraggled and she knew vaguely that the leeches were feeding on her again. She felt drugged by heat and fatigue and knew she looked a mess. When Falcon smiled at her she could barely respond.

'I'm okay,' she told him irritably when he voiced a note of concern. 'Just don't expect me to look like some cool Hollywood Jane out for an afternoon stroll with Tarzan.'

'You're doing fine.' Falcon gave her another smile of encouragement. 'Hollywood Janes they can keep on the film sets where they belong.'

It was about all the talking they did, for none of them had any energy to spare for idle conversation. They marched to the swish of disturbed foliage, the soft crunch of undergrowth, and the monotonous chop and hack of the parang. The canopy of trees had closed high above their heads, enveloping them in a world of moist green gloom.

Once they disturbed a troop of orangutans feeding in the upper branches, and paused to watch with envy as the ape-like figures swung away rapidly through the trees. Within less than a minute the shaggy orange fur of the last rearguard male had disappeared, at a speed which made their own slow rate of progress seem even more arduous.

They pushed on, sweating and struggling, slapping at insects. A dense thicket of thorns barred their way and they had to cut a path round it. They lost twenty minutes to gain half as many yards. Falcon consulted his compass constantly to keep them on course.

In any other circumstances he would have rested them in the fierce midday heat. But they couldn't afford to stop. This was now the third day since the plane had gone down. The survivors — if there were any survivors — must be desperate for rescue and medical aid. If possible he wanted to find them and get them back to the hovercraft before night fell again.

Gail was beginning to stagger, and even the Gurkhas were beginning to stumble occasionally and look a little bit weary, when at last they saw a break in the jungle ceiling ahead and above them. Falcon paused to look up with the rest and noted the jagged white splinters of broken branches where something large and heavy had smashed its way through the canopy of treetops.

He gripped Gail's arm, smiling at her, and feeling her come slowly alive with the almost unbelievable relief and hope.

'I think we've found it,' he said calmly.

He was right. They reached the point on the forest floor that was directly beneath the jagged opening to the brilliant blue sky, and from there followed the clearly marked trail of the aircraft's descent. The wings and engines had sheared off on either side, but the fuselage lay crumpled but almost intact a little more than a hundred yards from the point of entry. Their first sight of it was the tail fin, leaning at a drunken angle to starboard but protruding above the tangles of giant ferns and foliage which formed a secondary blanket below the forest giants and their trailing vines.

Corporal Ganju was in the lead with the parang, grinning with delight as he cleared the last few yards. They stopped beside the fuselage, staring around in all directions, and when the sound of their own movements ceased there was a heavy and ominous silence.

No haggard and unshaven survivors staggered out to meet them.

No faint voices cried for help.

There was nothing. No plane crew. No diplomats.

Just the long, sinister silence.

Falcon called out a loud hello, his voice echoing through the deepening gloom. A bird shrieked and a monkey crashed in panic through the distant branches, but there was no human answer.

Falcon frowned, and saw Gail's face take on a look of bitter disappointment. The first hope faded, and after a moment they spread out silently to look for bodies.

The passenger door into the fuselage had been torn off and Falcon was the first to go inside. The fuselage was broken and twisted at a slight angle near the tail, but the interior of the passenger cabin revealed very little damage. The seats were all in place, but empty except for the scattered items of light hand luggage which had been thrown off the overhead racks.

Falcon made his way forward. There were no pools of blood or splashes of brain matter, and he began to hope again that the majority of the VIP passengers had escaped unhurt. Perhaps they had moved away from the plane, trying to find their own way back to civilization.

Then he entered the flight deck.

And his briefly lifted hopes crashed for the second time.

There was a dead man at the controls, obviously the pilot. He had managed to avoid most of the giant tree trunks on the way down, but in the last seconds his luck had run out. The plane's nose was crushed inward against the monstrous girth of an ancient and moss-covered hardwood.

The pilot had probably died instantly, and it was not the sight of the badly crushed body which caused Falcon's hopes to plummet.

It was the more gruesome spectacle of the empty shoulders.

The pilot's head was missing, and it had not been torn off in the crash.

It looked more as though it had been severed neatly with a sharp blade.

There was a movement behind him. Falcon turned and saw Gail approaching up the aisle between the passenger seats. She had retrieved her medical bag from the Gurkhas and it was again slung over her right shoulder.

Falcon blocked the doorway into the flight deck.

'Steel yourself,' he warned her. 'There's nothing you can do, and it's not a pretty sight.'

She hesitated, bit her lip, and then pushed forward. Falcon gave her room.

'My God!' Her horror was controlled. 'Where's the head?'

'It's been removed.' Falcon wished he could give a more exact answer.

Gail looked at the shattered cockpit windows. 'Perhaps it was thrown out on impact.'

'Maybe.' Falcon didn't believe it, but if she wanted to think that then maybe for her it was best. He pulled at her arm.

'Let's get back outside. There's nothing for us in here.'

Gail nodded. She turned and led the way out. Falcon followed, his brain racing, wondering what in hell had happened here. His grip had tightened automatically on Kennard's Sterling and all his senses were on red alert.

They emerged from the fuselage and stood blinking for a moment in the broken rays of slanted sunlight. The Gurkhas had fanned out to search the area and as yet they knew of no reason to be quiet or cautious. The sound of their trampling feet and the familiar chopping of the parang were the only sounds Falcon could hear.

Then Bahadur Rama called his name sharply from the other side of the crashed plane.

They forced their way round the tail fin and found the Gurkha sergeant and one of his men crouched over a second body which lay belly down in a tangle of flowers and ferns. From the dark blue airline uniform Falcon recognized the co-pilot. Again the body had been separated from the head.

They found the third man of the flight crew, the radio operator, slumped against the bole of a palm tree a few yards away. Close by was the body of a young woman in a blue Malay sarong.

The final corpse the Gurkhas discovered was that of a small man in a light grey city suit. This one was further into the jungle, as though he had been trying to run away from the plane.

All of the bodies were headless.

And none of the heads could be found.

Gail was pale and tight-lipped, but she had come prepared to find some dead and mutilated bodies, so the shock was not total. She did her job and examined each body in turn. On two of the bodies she found crash injuries: the co-pilot had broken ribs and a broken arm, and the girl in the blue sarong had a badly gashed thigh that had been heavily bandaged.

All of them, except the pilot still at the controls, had walked out alive from the crash. They had been foully murdered some time later.

It was in the arm of the dead radio operator that she found the first bamboo dart. It was a thin sliver some nine inches long, feathered with a cone of soft balsa wood, the sharpened point embedded deep in the bicep muscle.

Gail reached to pull it out and Falcon's hand came down in an iron clamp around her wrist, stopping her while her fingers were still inches away.

'Don't touch,' he said grimly. 'It will be poisoned.'

Gail stared at him and then drew back. She hunted in her bag for her scissors and cut away the sleeves of the dead man's jacket and shirt, exposing the punctured flesh of the arm. It was discoloured, almost black.

'Ugh!' Gail looked as though at last she wanted to be sick.

They moved on and found a similar dart sticking out from under the left shoulder blade of the man in the grey suit.

'This must be one of the diplomats.' Gail spoke slowly, making a deliberate effort to steer her thoughts away from the obscene means of death. 'But which one?'

'It's not Sam Jordan.' Falcon was certain. He recalled a news picture of the Asian group taken outside the UN complex in New York and added, 'As far as I can remember both

Sumantri and Moreno were fairly tall men, so this must be Shinawatra, the Thai delegate.'

'And the woman?' Gail looked back towards the plane. 'Sumantri's wife?'

'Leila Sumantri was eight months pregnant,' Falcon reminded her. 'Mrs Chavan must be nearing sixty, and if she was wearing her national dress it would be a sari and not a sarong. The dead girl must be the stewardess.'

'Of course.' Gail was angry with herself for not having worked it out. Her thinking was blurred and Falcon knew that despite her outward show of calm she was inwardly badly shaken.

Bahadur Rama came toward them through the trees, his submachine gun unslung in his hands. All his men had their weapons at the ready.

'No more bodies, sah.' He reported grimly. 'And still no sign of heads. We have searched all round the plane. All heads taken away.'

Falcon frowned. 'So we have five people still missing, possibly alive — Jordan, Moreno, Sumantri and his wife, and the Indian woman, Kamala Chavan. All the diplomats gone, and all the plane crew dead!'

'Shinawatra is dead.' Gail glanced at the body again with repugnance.

'He tried to run.' Falcon was convinced of it. 'That was his mistake.'

Bahadur Rama squatted by the body. 'This native work, sah.' He offered helpfully.

'It looks that way,' Falcon acknowledged. The poison darts and missing heads all made up a positive picture. 'But I'm curious to know why they singled out the diplomats and took them alive.'

'If they are alive?' Gail said doubtfully.

'The people who did this had no use for dead bodies. The only trophies they collect are the heads.'

'The Dayaks?'

Falcon nodded. 'This *is* Borneo. The Dayak natives of the interior were once insatiable headhunters. We can only assume that they've reverted to type.'

'But the Dutch stamped out headhunting a hundred years ago.'

'True. But it revived again in World War Two. There are quite a number of Dayak longhouses with Japanese heads tucked away behind the rafters. Values get reversed in wartime. Killing becomes permissible again, approved and encouraged. Perhaps this was just another golden opportunity they felt they couldn't miss — or perhaps something has happened to make them think they're in some kind of restriction-free war situation again.'

'So why would they take prisoners? And how would they know how to single out the diplomats?'

'I don't know. The only answer is that someone with a bit more civilized know-how is using them.'

'Mark, none of this makes any sort of sense!'

'So far none of the things that have happened on this mission have made sense,' Falcon conceded grimly. 'But maybe we'll find some answers when we find those missing passengers.'

He turned to Bahadur Rama. 'Sergeant, get your men searching again. The Dayaks may be able to move through this jungle without leaving any trace. But the people from the plane were city people. They were made to walk and they must have left a trail. Find it. But make sure your men work in pairs. Each man to cover his partner's back.'

'Yes, sah!' Bahadur Rama saluted and withdrew to relay the new orders.

Falcon looked at Gail. 'Come on,' he said. 'We'll go back inside the plane.'

Gail didn't argue. A poisoned dart from a native blowpipe wouldn't be able to penetrate the steel fuselage, so obviously the interior of the plane was the safest place to be. She followed Falcon inside and slid down into the nearest passenger seat to rest. She felt drained, emotionally, mentally and physically, and it was with difficulty that she stopped herself from trembling. Five minutes passed before she was able to take any conscious interest in what Falcon was doing.

He was carefully examining the interior of the plane, working his way backward to the tail. He disappeared into the baggage compartment and after a while she pushed herself up and followed him.

'Mark, what are you looking for?'

'I think I've found it.'

Falcon showed her the severed ends of one of the control cables, and even her untrained eye could see that it had been partially sawn through with a hacksaw before it had broken.

'A bomb would have scattered the tailplane over a mile of jungle,' Falcon informed her calmly. 'So with the fuselage virtually intact it obviously wasn't a bomb. This was the next possibility to look for.'

'So it was sabotage!'

Falcon nodded. 'But I have a feeling the plane wasn't meant to come down here. Whoever weakened the cables probably calculated for it to come down further south, and disappear for ever to the bottom of the Java Sea. The hurricane caused extra stress and strain, and the cables parted too soon.'

Gail could only stare at him. Her brain was tired and she couldn't even work out the questions any more.

Falcon might have elaborated on his suspicions, but in that moment they heard a sharp warning in Nepalese. It was followed immediately by the unmistakable command tone of Bahadur Rama snapping orders.

Something was happening outside. Falcon moved past Gail and hurried to the exit with the Sterling submachine gun ready in his hands. He didn't cross the open doorway but went through low and fast and doubled back automatically into a crouch on the outside. Swiftly he scanned the new situation.

Bahadur Rama and his Gurkhas had their backs to him, fanned out around the plane, also crouching with their weapons levelled in a defensive circle.

The cause of their concern was instantly obvious. Three strangers had appeared, emerging calmly and unexpectedly from the jungle. They were not survivors from the plane and they were not Dayaks.

Two of them were either Malays or Javanese. The third was a white man, not too tall, but with powerful shoulders and a barrel chest, a rough, sun-burned face and shaggy, ginger-red hair.

All of them were dressed native style, in skirt-like sarongs, and all of them carried parangs in leather scabbards slung behind their backs.

Each man carried a rifle, and the rifles were the Russian-made AK-47.

CHAPTER 9

The rifles were not threatening, they were carried loosely, at arm's length in one hand, and none of them pointed at the plane. The three men looked surprised at their reception.

'Hey,' the red-headed man spoke with a slow, Texas drawl. 'It's okay. We're friendly.'

Bahadur Rama glanced back over his shoulder. 'Only these three, sah. I think!'

Falcon nodded acknowledgement. It checked out with his own reading. He straightened up and moved warily through the circle of Gurkhas.

'Who are you?' He asked bluntly.

'The name's Kraske.' The red-headed man grinned, a lopsided grin that looked as though his jaw might have been broken at some time and failed to mend properly. 'Steve Kraske. And don't be fooled by the skirt. I may have gone a little bit native, but I'm still all bull American.'

Falcon looked at the other two, deciding they were more Javanese than Malay. Kraske spoke up for them.

'These are my buddies. Yamin and Jusuf. They're okay. Number One, Gung-ho guys. I know them from a long way back.'

Yamin and Jusuf smiled. They were relaxed. They looked friendly. Falcon turned back to Kraske.

'How did you get here? What are you doing?'

'We came upriver in Yamin's boat. Then marched across country.' Kraske had decided to answer the questions as they came and he grinned again. 'As for what I'm doing, I reckon I must be doing the same as you — looking for a crashed plane.

I picked up the news on the radio, and figured maybe I ought to take a look and see what I could do to help.'

Gail had moved up behind Falcon. Her face was bewildered and she put in the next question.

'But what were you doing in this part of Borneo in the first place?'

Kraske looked surprised to see a woman, but it only gave another tilt to his smile. 'That's a long and involved story, Ma'am. Maybe I'll have the pleasure of telling it to you sometime. The end of the story is that I now have a trading post on the river. I guess I've found myself an outpost on the world's last wild frontier.'

'At Surajong?' Falcon was wary.

'No. Not on the Kiamba. The next river runs a parallel course about ten miles further east. The first town up from the delta is where I have my store.'

Kraske decided he had answered enough questions and pitched in one of his own. 'But how about you folks? I haven't seen anywhere a helicopter could land — so how did you get here?'

'We came up the Kiamba,' Gail explained. 'By hovercraft.'

'A hovercraft!' Kraske understood. 'So that's how you got here ahead of me. I was wondering how any rescue mission could get into the interior so fast. Hell, I could have saved myself the trip.'

He paused, then added. 'You have the advantage over me, Mister — you know my name.'

Falcon took the hint and introduced himself and his companions. Then he threw the last doubtful question.

'Where did you get the rifles — the A-K-Four-Sevens?'

Kraske glanced down at the weapon in his hand. He hefted it briefly as the grin of understanding came back.

'So that's what's bothering you. Don't let it. Before the purges the USSR poured a lot of guns and money into the PKI — that's the Indonesian Communist Party, or it was. A lot of those weapons are still left on Java. The Kalashnikov is a damned good rifle — my money says it's better than an American carbine — and they're easy to pick up.'

It was an explanation Falcon could accept. He had heard of American marines in Vietnam who had willingly swapped their M-16s for a captured AK-47. The American rifles had been known to jam in dirty combat conditions, the less sophisticated Russian rifles never did.

'It's okay,' he said to Bahadur Rama, and signed to the alert Gurkhas to lower their weapons. It was too soon to decide whether Kraske was telling the whole truth, but he presented no immediate danger so his story could only be taken at face value.

Kraske smiled as the tension was eased and turned his attention to the wrecked plane. He was puzzled by the silent and deserted fuselage. 'What happened to the crew and passengers?'

'The crew are all dead. Most of the passengers are missing.' Falcon watched Kraske's face but saw nothing readable as Kraske digested the information. Finally he offered: 'Come and take a look.'

He led the way round to the far side of the fuselage where the three crew bodies lay. Yamin and Jusuf and the ever-watchful Bahadur Rama followed behind Kraske.

Kraske looked startled when he saw the decapitated corpses. He swore and then spoke quickly with his two native companions in one of the Indonesian languages which Falcon did not understand. Then he switched back to English.

'This is Dayak work. The bloodthirsty little creeps are up to their old tricks. And they were here not too long ago. The vultures haven't found these bodies yet, and they can smell blood from a mile high.'

'How much do you know about the Dayaks?'

'Enough. They made headhunting a booming business in the past. They did so much of it they almost wiped themselves out. Every Dayak had to take a head to prove his manhood, to prove himself fit for marriage, or anything else you can think of. It was literally a way of life, with fresh heads needed for every ritual. They even buried heads with their dead, sometimes hundreds of heads, just to make sure that good old Grandad or whoever had plenty of slave servants in their idea of the hereafter.'

'So it's something basic to their traditions and beliefs.'

'That's right. And don't let any government official in Djakarta tell you it doesn't happen any more. There it's outlawed. Here it's different. Only now they usually wait until their betters are doing so much of their own political bloodletting that nobody notices. They had a head-collecting spree during World War Two. And another during the nationalist struggle against the Dutch which followed. They did it again during confrontation with Malaysia. And boy, did they have a ball when the communists were slaughtered wholesale in the purges that followed the failed PKI coup in sixty-five. That was one of the bloodiest massacres in world history, and it spread to every island in the archipelago — even Borneo. And while the Hindus and Muslims were getting their revenge on the communists, the Dayaks were paying off all their accumulated debts in heads. Every time they see they can get away with it, then out come the sacred *mandau* knives and they make up for the times when things are too peaceful and quiet.'

'You sound as though you've been around Borneo for a long time.'

'Yeah, Borneo, Bali and Java — for near on twenty years.' Kraske straightened up and looked Falcon squarely in the eyes. 'Maybe I'd best fill you in on some more of my past history, Mark. Then you can start trusting me.'

Falcon smiled. 'Go ahead,' he invited.

'Okay. Now I'm semi-retired, but when I first came out here I was working for the CIA. That was back in the early sixties. The war with Malaysia was hotting up, and at the same time Sukarno was courting with Peking and the PKI was building up to three and half million members which made it the biggest communist party outside the main bloc. A communist Indonesia combined with the communist military threat in Indo-China would have put the whole of South East Asia at risk, and Washington sure didn't want to see that.'

'So you were a spy?' Gail had come closer to listen and was trying to take it all in.

Kraske chuckled. 'They didn't call us spies, they called us military advisers. A lot of US military men worked in Vietnam in that role before they committed the marines, and a few of us CIA guys came into Indonesia. My job was with Yamin. He and his people are Muslims, and at that time he was leading a group of rebel guerrillas in an underground war against the PKI and the Sukarno government. I helped them with training and organization, and channelled in guns and other supplies.'

Kraske paused there and shrugged. 'There's a lot of stories I can tell — maybe when we're sitting in a bar somewhere over a beer. But that's it in a nutshell. After the troubles I settled down with a native wife. I married Yamin's sister, a real nice girl. That's why I stayed.'

It all sounded plausible, but Falcon wondered why Norville hadn't known anything about an ex-CIA man living native in this part of the world. Perhaps Kraske had been forgotten, he had said that he was semi-retired. In any case Falcon decided to initiate a check with Kuching as soon as they got back to the hovercraft and its radio. In the meantime he probed for any information Kraske might have on Surajong.

Kraske looked curious. 'That's twice you've asked about Surajong. What's so interesting about that crapheap of a place?'

Falcon told him how they had been ambushed.

Kraske frowned and scratched at his jaw. 'I don't figure it all, but I can guess why they're hostile. Surajong was one of the towns which sold itself body and soul to the PKI. When the purge came half the menfolk were butchered, in some cases their whole families as well. Most of those who survived were hauled off to the concentration camps as political prisoners. Some came back after five or six years, and if they haven't died the others are still rotting away.'

'But if there are no men left?' Gail was perplexed.

'That was fifteen years ago,' Kraske reminded her. 'A new generation of kids that were under teenage have since grown up into angry and bitter young men. They have bloody scores to settle, so I'd guess they just might be ready to support any new communist or terrorist movement that was anti-government.'

It was like filling in the clouds and sky in a jigsaw puzzle, some of the background was clear but the real picture was still missing. Falcon gave it a moment's thought, but then decided that if Kraske was genuine he was probably telling as much as he knew.

Time was vital and he turned to Bahadur Rama.

'Sergeant, did your men have any luck in finding that trail?'

'Yes, sah! This way!'

The white teeth gleamed under the fierce black moustache and he pointed back in the general direction of the ridge and the river.

Kraske said slowly, 'You plan to follow those missing passengers?'

Falcon nodded. 'That's what this mission is all about.'

'I'm sorry to say it, but you'll be wasting your time.' Kraske shrugged helplessly. 'Those people may have made a run for it, but they won't get far. The Dayaks will have caught up with them by now. They'll be just as dead and decapitated as the guys who got left behind.'

'I don't think they ran,' Falcon disagreed. 'They were taken away as prisoners.'

'That's not likely. The Dayaks wouldn't have any use for prisoners. Once they've started cutting heads off they won't want to leave any witnesses.'

Falcon had no time to argue. 'Either way I have to check it out.' He stated his position bluntly. 'My mission doesn't end until I find these people — alive or dead.'

Kraske looked undecided for a moment, but then he shrugged his broad shoulders.

'Okay. Now we know the headhunters are in action I still think there's no hope. But me and my buddies walked a long way on the same mission, so I guess we'll go along on the last stretch to help you finish it.'

CHAPTER 10

They moved off with no further delay, following the trail the Gurkhas had found. The keen-eyed Corporal Ganju led the way, proving himself an expert tracker and grinning cheerfully as he pointed out the clear marks of broken foliage, footprints and trampled ferns.

Falcon followed close behind Ganju, his Sterling ready for instant use as he searched the dense depths of jungle for any sign of life or movement on either side. He wanted to be in the lead to spot the first sign of trouble. Two of the Gurkha soldiers came next, then Gail, Kraske and his two companions, and finally the last soldier and Bahadur Rama bringing up the rear.

It was beginning to look now as though Peter Kennard could have been killed by a Dayak native after all, so at least there was no longer the acute fear of a traitor within their own group. Which meant that Falcon now felt safest with Bahadur Rama guarding the tail end of his column.

The trail was leading them north-east, and gradually veering more eastward, which gave them some comfort as they realized that they were making a rough circle back toward the river. It was easier going than the hard, direct path they had been forced to cut down from the ridge, for the Dayaks had taken the zigzag route of least resistance. It also meant that when they caught up with their quarry they would not have so far to walk back to the Kiamba and find the hovercraft, which gave another boost to their flagging spirits.

Also their party had been strengthened by three rifles. Kraske and his two companions looked to be capable men, all of them completely at home in the jungle, and their knowledge and experience could be an invaluable help.

Could be?

Falcon wished that he could get rid of the tiny, nagging doubt that still remained. Maybe it was the AK-47s. Kraske had provided a rational explanation, but the Kalashnikov was still the standard weapon of communist and terrorist groups throughout the world.

Or maybe it was something else. Perhaps Kraske was just too incredible a character to be real? Or perhaps his jack-in-the-box appearance in the middle of what should have been an empty jungle wilderness was just too convenient.

But Kraske was here. Good guy or bad guy, his presence would seem just as improbable, but the fact remained, he was here. Falcon had to accept it, but just the same he would stay on guard.

That was for sure. There was too much of the unexpected happening on this trip. So from now on he was going to be ready for anything that might happen next, every step of the way.

After two hours of hard travelling they arrived back at the ridge, at a point which Falcon calculated to be only two or three miles north of the point where they had left it. Here the trail became a clearly defined native footpath, leading north for a few hundred yards before it veered up and over the ridge.

They climbed out of the gloom of the jungle again, and Gail at least felt a deep sense of relief to be back in the open sunlight. The jungle was too dark and claustrophobic, and frightening now there was the fear of a headhunter lurking behind every tree. The air tasted better, fragrant with flowers instead of fungus and decay. Plus the insects were not so bothersome.

However, it was late afternoon and the daylight hours would soon be gone, so Falcon gave them only a few brief minutes to rest. Then they followed the continuing path which plunged down again into the dank gloom beneath the jungle canopy filling the Kiamba valley.

'We must be getting close.' Kraske moved up behind Falcon and warned him. 'The Dayak village will be near to the river. If you didn't see it then it must be a few miles up from where you parked your hovercraft.'

'That's the way I figure it,' Falcon agreed.

'This path must be a hunter's trail,' Kraske told him. 'They'll follow it into the jungle to hunt for game. They live by shooting down monkeys and birds with their blowpipes and darts. Then they have to cut the poisoned part of the meat out quick before it spreads and spoils the whole thing.'

Falcon nodded but did not prompt any more conversation. They needed to be quiet now and Kraske knew it too. He dropped back in the line and said no more.

The path joined up with another stream. At first Falcon thought it was the same one they had followed up from the lagoon, but then he realized it couldn't be. He wasn't that rusty. He knew his sense of distance and direction couldn't be that far out. This stream looked the same, but it would enter the Kiamba above the lagoon and the waterfall.

Falcon slowed the party down and moved with even more caution. As Kraske had pointed out, the Dayak village had to be sited near to fresh water. Which meant that it could be on the bank of the main river, or they could come upon it at any moment on the next twist of the narrow side stream.

They moved in silence except for the occasional snap of a twig or the rustle of foliage beneath Gail's feet. She was trying to tread quietly, but she didn't have the same jungle training as the rest of them. Falcon looked back once, frowning, but saw from the look of helpless anguish on her face that she was doing her best. He looked to his front again and said nothing.

He tried to calculate the odds on their approaching the village with any element of surprise. If a headhunter had killed Kennard then the tribespeople knew that the rescue party was in the area. But under the polished veneer of civilization his own primitive hunting instincts had been activated and sharpened by the years with S.A.S. and he was pretty sure that this far they were not being observed and trailed. Even if the Dayaks were invisible he would have sensed their presence.

Unless they were one hell of a lot better than the average guerrilla.

And perhaps they were. The Dayaks were a Stone Age people who had lived as part of the jungle since the dawn of time.

But they knew the risk of retribution, and if the main hunting party knew that a well-armed rescue mission was in the area they would have refrained from attacking the plane and taking heads.

Or would they? All speculation was useless and Falcon realized that in this situation it was no good trying to think like a chess player, or plan battle strategy like a general. He had to rely on those primitive instincts, stay sharp with all senses fine-tuned, and let his lightning reflexes deal with events as they came.

They had to be nearing the main river, and at last he saw the brightness of more sunlight at the end of the low green tunnel of dark leaves which framed the stream. Corporal Ganju, who was still in the lead, saw it in the same second and made a restraining, hold-back motion with his hand. Falcon stopped the column.

Ganju turned his head. The grin was missing. His face was serious. 'You want me to scout, sah?' he whispered softly.

Falcon hesitated, then decided that the little man could probably move more stealthily than he could move himself. He nodded.

Silent as a shadow, Ganju continued down the path. He was crouched low, placing his feet with infinite care, eyes moving constantly and listening after every step. He reached the point where the stream and the path opened out into the sunlight, and there he moved to the left of the path and vanished from their view.

Kraske and Bahadur Rama had moved up beside Falcon. Neither of them spoke. The whole column followed Falcon's example, kneeling and waiting in silence.

They became aware of the insects again, the aggravating buzz of flying ants, and the loud scratching of a beetle on a leaf. A large and brilliant blue butterfly skittered over the stream, and they heard bird calls sounding clear in the high tangles of branches and vines.

Falcon hoped that the birds were not transmitting warning signals that the Dayaks might recognize.

The minutes dragged by and the waiting got worse. They all became conscious of itches and bites they had managed to ignore before. A huge dragonfly hovered close to Gail's head, scaring her and causing her to cover her face with her arm. It stayed there, vibrating its wings and refusing to go away until she felt she wanted to scream.

Ten minutes passed. If Ganju had gone to his doom then it had happened quickly and silently. Perhaps a poisoned dart in the back of the neck. Falcon resisted the sudden need to ask Kraske whether the Dayak poison would have instantaneous effect.

The ten minutes became fifteen, and suddenly there was a shadow again at the far end of the stream tunnel. The little Gurkha corporal came padding back to rejoin them, showing his teeth again in a broken white gleam of reassurance.

His knowledge of English was limited, so he reported to Bahadur Rama in a long murmur of Nepalese. The sergeant listened without interruption and then relayed the information to Falcon.

'The village is about two hundred yards ahead, sah — where the stream meets the big river. Ganju says there is one very long hut, and some small huts. All the bad fellahs in the long hut. All prisoners must be there too.'

'Has Ganju seen them?'

'No, sah. He has crawled close under the long hut and heard bad fellahs talk. But plane people must be there too.'

'Sounds logical,' Kraske offered. 'They've had a long, hot hike through the jungle the same as we have. They'll put the prisoners in the longhouse, it's the communal gathering place where everything happens, and they'll be there with them, resting up. Anything they have planned for your plane passengers will take place when it gets cool in the evening.'

'What could they be planning?' Falcon asked.

Kraske shrugged. 'Well, sometimes they like to skewer an enemy on a twenty-foot pole and bury him still alive. They figure this gives power and strength to the bird of paradise which uses the end of the pole that's left sticking up as a take-off point for carrying the souls of their dead up to heaven.'

Gail hugged herself and shuddered.

Falcon merely frowned. Kraske's knowledge of Dayak ritual could explain why the headhunters had taken prisoners, but not why they had been so selective in singling out the diplomats and rejecting the plane crew.

However, he had to put that problem aside and return to the job that was most urgent. He cleared a patch of the leaf and mould carpet to expose an area of clear dirt, and with a stick drew in the stream and the river. Then he asked Ganju to add the layout of the Dayak village.

The little Gurkha scratched quickly and confidently, and the finished diagram showed the longhouse on the junction with river, with four smaller huts strung out in a continuing line along the riverbank, and a fifth hut tucked back a little way from the mouth of the stream.

Falcon studied it for a moment and then ordered quietly: 'Sergeant, take the Gurkhas round to the far end of the village. When you're in position, fire a good burst over the huts and then rush into the longhouse. I'll come in from this end. They only have bows and arrows and blowpipes so the warning gunfire should demoralize them. Get in fast, before they can get their wits together, and it shouldn't be necessary to kill any of them.'

Bahadur Rama looked a little bit disappointed with the note of restraint, but he nodded understanding.

Kraske said doubtfully. 'I guess my boys had best stay back with Doctor Crawford. Mark, I'll go with you.'

Falcon wasn't sure that he wanted the company, but it was a difficult offer to refuse. He nodded agreement.

Gail looked a bit reluctant at being left behind with two strangers, but Yamin and Jusuf gave her reassuring smiles and she made no protest. She watched as the others moved along the stream to the sunlight, and hoped that the rescue would be over quickly so that she could follow them out of the darkening gloom.

When they reached the clearing the village appeared to be deserted, except for a twist of smoke curling up from a hole in the roof of the longhouse. Falcon guessed it was from a cooking fire. The nearest of the small huts was clearly in view, but the others were half obscured by palm fronds and foliage. Falcon watched and listened for a few minutes, and then signed to Bahadur Rama to proceed.

In single file, silent as ghosts, the Gurkhas moved off along one of the paths that Ganju had already scouted around the edge of the village.

Falcon gave them five minutes, watching and listening. Very faintly he could hear the mutter of native voices from inside the longhouse, but no native showed himself. Finally he glanced at Kraske and nodded toward the small square hut, raised a few feet from the ground, which was nearest to them.

They moved silently, flitting across a patch of open, crudely cultivated ground to the back of the hut. Falcon listened with his ear against the grass- and palm-frond thatch, always double-checking. There was no sound and he signed to Kraske again. They moved up on either side of the hut, met again at the front and ducked into the black shadow of the doorway.

They were fifteen yards from the end of the longhouse, and now able to see it clearly. The building was about fifty feet long, constructed from rough-hewn timbers and roofed with thatch and wooden shingles. It stood about eight feet above the ground on a forest of stilts, and a notched log served as a ladder leading up to the verandah which ran the whole length of the building facing over the river.

They waited another two minutes before the pregnant stillness was abruptly desecrated by the simultaneous crash of five submachine guns firing rapidly into the air.

Falcon moved like a sprinter at the sound of a starting pistol, running forward and hauling himself swiftly up the stepped pole. It was no more difficult than a military assault course, but as he reached the verandah a screaming Dayak charged at him swinging a vicious parang.

Falcon saw a wild little man with straight black hair, naked except for a loincloth, and heavily tattooed with black and blue decorations. His black eyes were filled more with terror than with rage, but the parang was a lethal weapon and Falcon had no choice. He triggered the Sterling and sent the Dayak cartwheeling backwards off the verandah.

Bahadur Rama appeared at the far end of the building, his soldiers pulling themselves up quickly onto the verandah behind him. The Gurkha sergeant vanished through a dark doorway into the longhouse with the rest at his heels.

More submachine gun fire blazed inside the longhouse. It was filled with an inhuman screaming, and then — Falcon froze — the unmistakable crackle of Kalashnikovs.

Falcon spun on his heel. Kraske was climbing onto the verandah behind him, his rifle not yet levelled. Their eyes met and held. Falcon uncertain. Kraske looking the same.

Falcon had thought instantly of Jusuf and Yamin, but then he realized there were more than two of the distinctive AK-47s being used. He spun back again as another Dayak warrior came stumbling out of the nearest doorway. The headhunter carried a rifle but didn't fully understand how to use it. He fumbled with the trigger and shot off half his own foot, then collapsed screeching on the verandah.

Falcon kicked the AK-47 into the river, stepped over the squirming body, and dived into the longhouse.

Inside was semi-darkness and total confusion. Dayak men, women and children were screaming and running in all directions. Two women carrying babies ran straight at Falcon and he moved aside and let them continue their flight through the doorway. Most of the men seemed to have grabbed for a weapon, a blowpipe or a parang, but at least six of them were struggling with the unfamiliar rifles. One managed to shoot one of his own companions before a Gurkha Sterling cut him down. The others gave up and threw the weapons away.

It was over in a very few minutes. The headhunters with parangs proved themselves the more dangerous and two of them had to be killed. The rest either vanished through holes in the floor, or threw themselves down whimpering.

Falcon straightened up, his eyes adjusting quickly to the gloom, and surveyed the damage.

In that second a Kalashnikov was fired behind him.

Falcon whirled round and a poisoned dart smacked into the wooden post beside his head.

Kraske was smiling, the muzzle of his rifle curled smoke. He used it to point and Falcon turned again and looked upward.

A blowpipe fell at his feet, and the last resisting Dayak warrior tumbled slowly out of the roof rafters to follow it down.

CHAPTER 11

Bahadur Rama and his Gurkhas quickly rounded up the Dayak villagers and moved them out of the longhouse onto the riverbank where they could be more closely watched. They were mostly women, children and old men, badly frightened and blinking miserably in the sunlight. Five of their men had been killed, but most of the others had managed to slip away. The women wailed their grief over the bodies and the babies cried.

Falcon was angry. His face was tight-lipped and cold.

He was not angry with the huddled group of dejected Dayaks, but with whoever had supplied the village with modern weapons. The little warriors had not even known how to aim straight, but the rifles had given them false hope and false courage. Perhaps they believed they had been given the same *magic* as the attacking enemy. But all it had brought them was an unwanted death toll when the killing should not have been necessary.

Bahadur Rama was apologetic. His men had come out of the battle without a scratch, but if they had hesitated and held back when the Kalashnikovs opened fire there would almost certainly have been casualties.

Falcon could not blame the Gurkhas.

But he could and did blame the political animals who sought to further their own ruthless cause by putting sophisticated arms into the hands of an easily-impressed people. Whoever they were, and whatever their cause, they had brought disaster to the Dayaks. But they probably considered them as expendable anyway.

On the credit side they had rescued the survivors from the plane crash. The three men and two women had been kept at one end of the longhouse, where they had the good sense to keep themselves pressed flat to the floorboards while the shooting was in progress.

When it was over and the Gurkhas had cleared out the natives, three of the plane passengers came forward. In the lead was the American from the US State Department, a tall man in his mid-fifties with iron-grey hair and square, horn-rimmed glasses. Falcon recognized Sam Jordan before the other man introduced himself. Jordan was in line for an Undersecretary post, his face was often in the news, and he was considered the most capable Asia expert in the Department. He looked reasonably fit, despite his ordeal, and his welcoming handshake was firm.

Behind him was a very tall, thin man with an aquiline nose dominating his Spanish features. A bloody bandage was tied around his head. He was Luis Moreno, the Filipino delegate.

Moving more slowly was a grey-haired woman in her sixties. The now muddied but once expensive blue silk sari identified her as the Indian delegate. It was said that Kamala Chavan was as tough as old boots, and out of the same mould as the indomitable Mrs Gandhi. She looked tired, the wrinkled bags under her old eyes were heavy, but she was surprisingly buoyant.

'No, I am not hurt,' she assured Falcon calmly. 'The past three days have been most unpleasant, but I have been on election campaigns which were nearly as bad.'

'Well, at least three of you can walk,' Falcon said with some relief. 'What about the others?'

'Mrs Sumantri can walk,' Jordan told him. 'But Doctor Sumantri will have to be carried. He's got a busted leg.'

They moved to the end of the longhouse where a slim Javanese girl in a sarong was crouched over a crude litter of ropes and branches which contained her injured husband. She looked up with large, long-lashed and tear-stained eyes, and even in the gloom, and despite the haggard lines of strain on her face, Falcon could see that she was beautiful. Sumantri was conscious but grey with pain.

'Luis and I had to carry him from the crash site,' Jordan explained. 'Luckily we had the litter all made up ready. We figured we were gonna need one if anybody ever found us, and it gave us something positive to do while we waited. But it was a rough ride for him. He's had a bad time.'

'We've got a doctor to take a look at him,' Falcon assured them. 'Medicine, not philosophy.' He called to Bahadur Rama and ordered a Gurkha to be sent back up the path to fetch Gail.

While they waited for her to come up they carried Sumantri's litter out onto the riverbank. There they quickly exchanged stories.

'It poured with rain for two days after the plane crashed,' Jordan said. 'Maybe that was in our favour. There was so much water falling that any spark or flame that might have appeared on impact must have been immediately flooded out. Anyway, there was no fire. The weather cleared early this morning, so that's when we got out and made the stretcher. The plane crew were hoping to see a rescue mission arrive, but they knew that even a helicopter wouldn't be able to land anywhere close to us. Then, at about midday, the natives found us.'

'We saw the crash site,' Falcon filled in. He could see from Leila Sumantri's face that she had no wish to relive the full, gory details. 'We know what happened there.'

He went on to give a brief account of their own expedition, ending on a note of comfort. 'We should be able to get back to the hovercraft before dark, and that means back on board *Scotsman* before morning.'

Gail had come hurrying up with Yamin and Jusuf trailing behind. Quickly she unslung her medical bag and began checking over her new patients.

Sumantri's thigh bone was broken, but the injured leg had been bandaged in splints and then strapped to the sound leg for support. The job had been done as well as could be expected by Jordan and the short-lived co-pilot.

'There's nothing to be gained by interfering with it now,' Gail decided. 'When we get him back it will have to be X-rayed, and then if necessary re-set in an operating theatre with the proper facilities.' She looked up into the worried face of Leila Sumantri and smiled. 'In the meantime I can give him a shot to dull the pain, and some quinine to bring down the fever. He's going to be okay.'

She finished ministering to Sumantri, and then re-dressed the lacerated scalp wound for Moreno. While she worked Falcon conferred briefly with Kraske and Jordan.

At Falcon's insistence Kraske made a vain attempt to question the Dayaks, trying several Indonesian languages and dialects, and finally calling on Yamin and Jusuf who also had no success. Either the villagers did not understand what was being asked of them, or they were too shocked or sullen to make any response.

Giving it up Falcon and Kraske went back into the longhouse, looking for some clue to the origin of the unexpected Kalashnikov rifles. They found nothing, but as they turned to leave Kraske stopped and pointed upward.

Falcon looked up into the gloom where the rafters supported the thatch and shingle roof. He saw a gruesome row of age-discoloured heads, all suspended by strands of hair. And then the five fresh heads.

'I guess the guy who blew the last dart at you was arranging the new trophies when the Gurkhas busted in,' Kraske said casually. 'Lucky for you I spotted him. I reckon I spoiled his aim.'

Falcon nodded. 'Thanks,' he said, and felt uncomfortable. He still harboured vague suspicions about Kraske, but he had to admit that they didn't fit in with the guy saving his life.

They went outside again. Gail had finished her medical checks and came to meet them.

'We have to get moving,' she advised. 'But slowly. I don't think Mrs Chavan is quite the tough old bird she makes herself out to be. And Leila Sumantri is so far pregnant it's an absolute miracle that she hasn't already suffered a miscarriage.'

Falcon nodded and gave the necessary orders.

They moved out, with two of the Gurkhas carrying Sumantri's litter. Falcon led the way, and again he posted the reliable Bahadur Rama at the tail end of the column. They followed the main course of the river downstream, and fortunately there was another well-used path which made the going fairly easy.

There was nothing to do with the Dayaks except leave them behind. Falcon could not afford to burden his small party with prisoners, and even if the hovercraft had been capable of carrying the extra weight any idea of dragging a few scapegoats back to face courtroom justice would have been both repugnant and pointless. The warriors who had committed the head-cutting crimes had either been killed or had escaped, and the village as a unit had paid dearly for its sins.

However, he took the precaution of throwing all their weapons, from blowpipes to Kalashnikovs, far out into the fast-flowing Kiamba. He kept just one of the Russian rifles as evidence, and in the hope that once they had returned to Kuching there might be some means of tracing its route and its purpose in the wild heartland of central Borneo.

It was late in the day. Falcon guessed a couple of hours of daylight left at the most, then the swift, almost instant sunset. But with luck it would be enough for them to get back to the hovercraft before darkness.

He calculated they had a three- or four-mile march at the most. They were all weary and hungry, but now the rush and swirl of the river beside them was a positive encouragement. It assured them they were not lost, and that they were moving in the right direction.

The jungle hung low over the path, slapping at their bodies and faces, and sometimes blotting out the green flow of the river, although they could always hear its sound. The sandflies and other airborne insects thickened up and became more of a nuisance as dusk approached, but at least they were through the boiling heat of midday.

Twice they heard the sinister splash of crocodiles slithering into the river ahead of them, and once a huge flock of bats came hurtling upriver in a flapping black cloud. To Gail the bats were more repugnant than the crocodiles, which they never actually saw.

They moved slowly, letting the Indian woman and Leila Sumantri set the pace, but after the first mile Gail caught up with Falcon and reluctantly called him to a halt.

'I'm sorry, Mark — but this is no good. The baby is too near and Mrs Sumantri was exhausted before we started. We'll have to make another litter and carry her.'

Falcon looked back and saw that Leila Sumantri's face was very pale and drawn, her brow beaded with perspiration. She was holding her distended belly with both hands, as though trying to support the extra weight.

'You're the doctor,' he acknowledged Gail. 'Whatever you say, goes.' He called up Bahadur Rama and gave orders for the Gurkhas to fashion another litter.

Kraske spoke to his two companions and they gave the lead in cutting down the necessary branches and vines. Clearly it was a job they had done before. While they worked, Kraske relaxed with Gail and the thankful diplomats. All of them were glad to sit down by the path and rest.

Falcon remained standing, moving back down the path a little way to keep watch, but staying within hearing.

After a minute Jordan had got his breath back. He was curious about Kraske and began asking questions. Kraske did not seem perturbed and told his incredible story over again.

'That's just fascinating,' Jordan said at last. 'During the late fifties and early sixties I was working with our embassy in Taiwan. I met a lot of guys like you — CIA case officers working with the anti-communist forces in the Philippines and Indonesia. Did you ever pass through Taiwan?'

Falcon wondered afterward if he had imagined the brief hesitation before Kraske answered.

'No. My jump-off point was Manila. I never did get to Taiwan. I went into Java and worked there for a couple of years. Then I got assigned to Yamin's group. That was in sixty-three. Sukarno had twelve thousand men in Borneo, making terrorist raids over the borders into Sabah and Sarawak. And the PKI was strong in Sukarno's army. Yamin and his Muslim group were fighting Sukarno and the PKI, but they needed a supply chain set up.'

'I wasn't supposed to know about it,' Jordan mused. 'But I seem to remember we sent some pretty good Nationalist Chinese agents into Sumatra. You ever meet up with any of those guys?'

'I don't think so. The Sumatra rebellion was in fifty-eight. At that time I was still on Java. Later, when I teamed up with Yamin in Borneo, we got kinda isolated from the rest of the Indonesia picture.'

'Yeah,' Jordan said. 'Indonesia is a confusing area, all those different islands, it was kinda hard to keep track of it all.'

Gail got curious again. 'How did you live?' she asked. 'I mean if you were all rebels fighting in the jungle, then what did you eat? All I saw in that Dayak village was some rotting fish, and what looked like a stewed monkey. It smelled revolting.'

Kraske chuckled. 'There's more than that in Borneo. The jungle is full of durian and other edible fruits. Some of the birds make good eating, and for big meat we used to shoot ape, plenty of wild pig, and sometimes a Borneo bear. Those bear steaks were real good.'

Falcon wished that Gail had not interrupted and waited for Jordan to speak again. But the conversation was over. A scream and a violent commotion in the jungle brought it to an abrupt end.

Falcon sprinted to the scene, and found Kraske's man Jusuf writhing in agony in the undergrowth. For a moment he thought the unfortunate man had been snake-bitten, for the jungle was full of kraits, cobras, and other venomous species. Then Yamin ran up and turned his friend over.

They both stared at the thin sliver of wood-feathered bamboo embedded in Jusuf's throat.

Jusuf was dead within two minutes.

Falcon quickly deployed the Gurkhas to protect the diplomats, although there was no sign of any further danger. Jusuf had moved away from the rest of the party in his search for the most pliable vines, and the Dayak warrior who had killed him had vanished again into the green curtains of leaf and gloom without leaving a single trace.

Yamin was furious, his face anguished, and he argued angrily with Kraske before Kraske snapped back at him to shut him up. Their talk was in Javanese and Falcon was frustrated because he couldn't understand it. He was fluent in most European languages and had mastered some Arabic and Russian, but the wide variety of Indonesian languages were beyond his experience.

Kraske finally returned to English.

'Those little bastards must have rallied more quickly than I expected. But I guess I should have known. They'll want revenge, and they've got dead to bury. They'll need more bloody heads to send them on their way with full honours.'

Falcon frowned. He felt that he was at fault too for underestimating the Dayaks. And the knowledge that the little headhunters who had been able to escape with their weapons were now stalking them through the jungle sent a cold chill down the nerve centres in his spine.

The thought of dying from the swift, silent poison was somehow even more unnerving than the prospect of being shot at with bullets.

He said grimly, 'I'm sorry, Steve. There's nothing we can do for Jusuf. And now we have even more need to make haste and get back to the hovercraft.'

'You can give me a couple of minutes,' Kraske said bitterly. 'Because we're not leaving him here so they can come back and take his head after we've gone. We'll feed him to the goddamned crocs first.'

Falcon hesitated, and then nodded. He went back to the main party, soothed the diplomats as well as he was able, and speeded up the Gurkhas on the task of constructing the second litter.

In the meantime Kraske and Yamin carried the limp body of their friend to the riverbank. They stood there for some minutes and argued again with bitter voices. Then they reached agreement and picked up the body once more. They swung it twice and then hurled it far out into the centre of the river, where the green floodwaters carried it swiftly away.

They watched it out of sight, then came slowly back to rejoin the main party. Kraske looked bleak. Yamin's face was hard-set and sullen.

They continued the march, with the Gurkhas carrying the two litters, and after another hour they came to the waterfall. The shadows were lengthening, with darkness filling the deeper recesses of the jungle when they at last heard the roar of the river plunging over the short but sheer drop.

They moved more slowly as they descended the steeply stepped path between the huge boulders beside the falls. At this stage Falcon was not risking any accidents, and he made them take every step with care.

They reached the lagoon safely and there another unexpected shock awaited them.

The lagoon was empty.

The two Gurkha soldiers they had left to guard the hovercraft were sprawled dead on the narrow mud beach.

Tom Harris and the SRN5 had disappeared.

CHAPTER 12

For a moment the whole party stood motionless in the gathering gloom. There was no sound but the muted roar of falling water, the croak of a frog, and the ever-present buzz of insects. Then slowly the Gurkhas lowered the two litters and unslung their submachine guns. Their faces were suddenly stiff, almost wooden, as they smothered their emotions.

Falcon moved forward with Bahadur Rama to examine the two dead soldiers. He expected to find more of the poisoned bamboo darts, but the two guards had not been killed by primitive stealth. Instead they had been cut down by automatic gunfire. One body had three bullet holes in the chest. The other had been shot in the head and shoulder.

There were drag marks across the mud where the second body had been pulled toward the edge of the lagoon. The extended right leg was bloodied by jaw marks, and Falcon guessed that their return had disturbed a crocodile from making off with a free meal.

Gail came to join them, carrying her medical bag, but there was nothing she could do. She bit her lip and said nothing.

Kraske and Jordan followed her. Jordan looked stunned and disappointed. He waited for somebody to say something. Kraske still looked bitter and he was the one who spoke first.

'More Dayak work. The little bastards are sure moving fast.'

'No.' Falcon did not agree.

Kraske looked at the obvious bullet wounds and shrugged. 'They had rifles as well as blowpipes.'

'I remember. But they hardly knew the muzzle end from the butt. The Gurkhas are first-class soldiers, which means that whoever wiped them out had to be fast and good, and proficient with the weapons they were using.'

He paused and looked out over the black pool of the lagoon. 'In any case there's no way the Dayaks could have hidden the hovercraft. It could only be moved under its own power, and that means someone who could figure out how to start the engine and use the controls.'

Gail looked to where the river vanished into the forest, the only way the hovercraft could have gone.

'What's happened to Tom?' She asked in a weak voice.

Falcon was asking himself the same question. There was only the one drag mark on the mud, so Harris had obviously not been killed on the beach with the others. It was possible he had been shot and toppled straight into the lagoon, but if Harris was dead, then who could have moved the hovercraft?

'Perhaps your friend took the hovercraft back downriver,' Kraske offered. 'He may have gone for help — or maybe he just ran out on you.'

Falcon considered the possibilities. An unknown enemy had attacked the beach, killing Harris and the Gurkhas, and someone on the other side had enough know-how to drive the hovercraft away. Or Harris had survived to drive off in the hovercraft, either in the hope of getting back to *Scotsman* to get help, or just to abandon them.

Or there was a third alternative.

Falcon had been right the first time when he had suspected a traitor inside their own party, and wrong when he had later decided that the murder of Peter Kennard had been committed by a hostile Dayak. There had been a traitor. Tom Harris. Harris could have killed Kennard, and later gunned down the two unsuspecting Gurkhas in order to leave them all to the merciless attentions of the natives.

But how would Harris know they had encountered the Dayaks? And why should the British sergeant be working against them?

Falcon shook his head irritably as the questions came full circle with no satisfactory answers. Then he looked to Bahadur Rama.

'Have your men scout the immediate area. See if you can find Sergeant Harris — or anything that might shed some light on this mess.'

'Yes, sah.' The snap had temporarily gone out of Bahadur Rama's voice, and his face was expressionless as he walked away. Falcon watched him go and knew the Gurkha sergeant would make an implacable enemy. If they ever found Tom Harris alive then Harris would have some pretty fast explaining to do.

'What happens now?' Sam Jordan asked the question, speaking up for the bewildered and exhausted survivors from the plane.

Night had fallen and they couldn't go on. Even if they had the strength and could find the riverbank path, the Dayaks would find them easy prey as a straggling line in the darkness.

'We'll have to camp here,' Falcon decided. 'Then at daybreak I guess we'll have no choice but to start walking again.'

'Where to?'

Falcon looked at Kraske. 'You said you had a boat on the next river. What are our chances of walking across country to reach it?'

'Carrying two stretchers, no hope at all. It's fifteen miles of leg-breaking jungle, with two steep mountain ridges and half a dozen ravines to get up and down.'

'So we'll have to stay on the Kiamba, and walk all the way to Surajong. There we should be able to buy, beg, or steal some kind of river transport.'

'But Surajong is hostile!' Gail said helplessly.

'Maybe not the whole town. Maybe just elements of it.' Falcon was tired but he forced a smile. 'Don't worry, I'll go in alone to check it out. If it looks bad I'll forget about buying or begging, and just go straight to stealing.'

'I guess we don't have any real choice,' Kraske agreed. 'But tonight we're gonna have to post guards to keep those goddamned Dayaks from getting too close. You can count on me and Yamin to take our turn.'

'Thanks,' Falcon said cautiously. 'We'll have to take turns in pairs, so Yamin can stand guard with Sergeant Rama, and you can share a watch with me.'

Kraske hesitated, and then nodded. His eyes were unreadable.

If he had any objection to being split up from Yamin, Kraske was keeping it quiet. But without the hovercraft radio Falcon had no way of checking up on Kraske's life story, and he was still taking no unnecessary chances.

It was a subdued camp. The day had been long and hard, the sweat-sucking heat had been murderous, and with the seemingly endless succession of sudden, violent shocks it had left them all limp with fatigue. They were all hungry, but there was nothing left of their emergency rations, their main supplies had been left with the hovercraft, and now that night had fallen it was too dark to hope to shoot game.

The Gurkhas demolished one of the ancient, abandoned native huts, and used the dry thatch and timbers to light a large fire on the edge of the lagoon. It was not cold, but the flames gave some cheer and comfort, and at least they would keep away the crocodiles, and enabled Corporal Ganju to brew up a last pot of tea.

In the cleared square where the hut had been Bahadur Rama and his men dug deep and buried their murdered comrades.

Gail made the rounds of her patients, and pronounced them no worse than when they had been discovered in the Dayak longhouse. However, she was worried about Sumantri's leg, and about the general condition of the others.

She came to sit by Falcon and asked doubtfully, 'Do you really think we can carry two stretchers all the way to Surajong? Or that old Mrs Chavan can walk that far?'

'I've been having second thoughts about it,' Falcon admitted. 'I think that if we can get them down the river past the rapids, then perhaps we will build a raft. We can cut steering poles and let the river carry us the rest of the way.'

'How long will it all take?'

'A few days if we are lucky. The river is running fast after all the rains, so it all depends on how long it takes us to get below the rapids.'

Gail shook her head slowly. 'I don't think Leila Sumantri's baby will wait that long.'

'But you can cope.' Falcon made a shrug of his shoulders. 'You have delivered babies before. And perhaps it will be best. If Leila has the baby, then someone else can carry it.'

Gail stared at him, the reflected light of the flames suddenly glinting in the honey-brown eyes. Falcon recognized his own mistake and quickly reached to take her hand.

'I did not mean to sound callous,' he apologized. 'Only practical. It will be easier for one of the Gurkhas to carry Leila's baby, than for two of them to have to carry Leila, the baby, and a stretcher.'

Gail slowly relaxed. 'You're right. I'm sorry, Mark, I'm just so damned edgy.'

Her hand stayed in his, she made no attempt to remove it. Instead she relaxed further and leaned her head on his shoulder. They were silent for a moment before she turned her face to look up at him.

'I hope you don't mind. But it's been a hell of a day.'

'It's okay.' Falcon moved his arm around her to make her more comfortable. He smiled and added softly, 'When we get back to some form of civilization, I must find ways to make it up to you.'

She returned the smile, her face suddenly hopeful and knowing in the firelight. Her eyes were now soft and gleaming, and full of rich, sweet promises of their own.

There was only a minimum of talk around the campfire. Falcon had hopes that Jordan might engage Kraske in another probing conversation, but like the rest of them Jordan was weary. With nothing more substantial than one cup of the weak tea each there was nothing to keep them awake. They were fearful of the crocodiles in the lagoon and the Dayaks in the jungle, but they made themselves as comfortable as possible on the hard mud beach. Sleep washed over them as a blessed relief to numb minds and aching muscles.

Falcon was the last to relax. He sat with his back against the log they had been using as a seat. His submachine gun leaned ready to hand against his right knee, and Gail's head was pillowed by his left thigh.

For an hour he watched, listened, and waited. The jungle was alive with the croaking chorus of frogs, and occasionally there was the splash of something bigger and more sinister further downriver, but nothing ventured out of the water to threaten the huddled figures around the fire.

The two Gurkhas he had posted to take the first watch stayed alert, changing their positions silently from time to time, either to put more wood on the flames, or simply to stay awake. The little Nepalese had worked hard throughout the day, so Falcon had paired them on the first and last watches of the night so that they could get the maximum hours of unbroken sleep.

Bahadur Rama and Yamin would take the next watch. And then Falcon and Kraske.

Finally Falcon decided he could trust the Gurkhas. Also he had the feeling that if there were any headhunters still stalking the party, then they would have attempted to claim another victim soon after the party had settled for the night, or they would wait until the first light of dawn.

He closed his eyes to sleep, but it seemed that he had only slowed his breathing for a few brief minutes before a firm hand was pulling at his shoulder. He opened his eyes and saw the strained face of Bahadur Rama.

'Sah. Corporal Ganju has gone missing!'

Falcon sat up and reached for his Sterling. Behind the sergeant he saw the two Gurkhas who had been on watch.

'What happened?' he demanded.

'Sah, these two wake me to take my turn. I notice Ganju's place for sleeping is empty. The guards say he got up perhaps ten minutes ago. He went into jungle — they think to urinate. They did not notice he had not come back.'

'Have you looked for him?'

'Yes, sah.' Bahadur Rama ground his teeth in frustration. 'We find nothing. Ganju just disappear.'

Falcon swore angrily, for if the Gurkhas had already searched and found nothing then there was no more to be done until dawn. It would be hopeless and dangerous for them all to continue blundering around the jungle in the pitch darkness.

'Goddamnit,' he growled. 'Ganju should have known better than to go off the beach on his own.'

One of the soldiers volunteered some more information in Nepalese. Bahadur Rama translated.

'Sah, he says Kraske's man Yamin went into the jungle ahead of Ganju. Yamin came back. Ganju did not.'

Falcon frowned, and all his former suspicions flooded back. Yamin was due to stand watch with Bahadur Rama, so it was time to wake him anyway. When they did so Yamin blinked and yawned, and looked up at them innocently.

Falcon tried to question him but the Javanese simply looked blank, showing no sign of understanding. However, the low voices disturbed Kraske who came to ask what was happening.

Falcon put his questions again through Kraske, and received some predictably unhelpful answers.

Yamin admitted that he had gone into the forest to urinate a short time before, but insisted that he had not passed the Gurkha corporal on his way back. He had not seen or heard anything to cause him any alarm.

Kraske voiced the opinion that the Dayaks had taken another head.

Falcon was not so sure.

He was a long way from being satisfied, but he was back in the maddening situation of having no means of determining the truth. Kraske and Yamin could yet prove to be guiltless allies — or an extremely dangerous fifth column.

It was a toss-up, and he didn't even have a coin to spin.

CHAPTER 13

They passed through another crisis before dawn, for in the early hours of the morning Leila Sumantri's baby was born. Gail handled the delivery with help from Mrs Chavan. The Indian woman had had six children of her own before entering politics, and despite her own acute weariness she proved a solid comfort and support. The practical, down-to-earth, I'll-help-you-but-I'll-stand-no-nonsense approach, which had raised four daughters and two sons and endeared her in later years to the Indian electorate, again proved an invaluable asset at the jungle birth.

The baby's first cries greeted the sunrise. It was a boy, and like a good omen for its future a bird of paradise flew in the same moment over the still water of the lagoon.

Leila needed time to rest, and to share her joy with her husband, so Falcon used the time to lead another search for the missing Corporal Ganju. However, they found nothing, except a trail of broken undergrowth leading to the river. It might have been made by a dragged body during the night, or by the passage of a crocodile the day before.

Falcon studied the marks carefully, going over them twice, but in the end he was again frustrated. They were inconclusive, and the only certainty he knew was that the members of his party were being steadily whittled away.

First Peter Kennard. Then the two Gurkha soldiers and Tom Harris. Now the skinny little corporal who would grin his cheerful grin no more.

And who next?

And by whom? The stalking Dayaks? The unidentified hostile forces at Surajong? Or by a two-faced enemy within their own depleted ranks?

He had his suspicions but no proof.

Somehow he had to find the answers before it was too late and there were none of them left.

The plane crash survivors looked equally worried. The horrors and narrow escapes from death they had endured, together with the prospect of the dangers and the hardships still to come, had combined to test their courage to the limit. Moreno looked sick and nervous. Leila was very weak. And Sumantri was a man filled with mental and physical anguish, he was pained by his leg and fretted over the health of his wife and newborn son. The baby was premature and underweight.

Only Kraske seemed relatively unconcerned. He had lived in and off the jungle before, and at least had no basic fears of starvation or dying of thirst. He found them a spartan breakfast of wild durian fruits and a few large green coconuts, and promised that sometime during the day's march he would shoot something more substantial for the pot.

'Not monkey,' Gail begged, and Kraske roared with laughter.

It eased some of the tension and Falcon took advantage of the moment to get them organized to move out.

Their Gurkha escort had now been reduced to three soldiers, plus Bahadur Rama. Just enough to carry the two stretchers, but leaving no one to bring up the rearguard whom Falcon could fully trust. Perhaps later in the day Leila Sumantri would recover some of her strength, but it was too soon to expect her to walk.

Falcon finally decided to give the AK-47 he had brought from the Dayak village to Sam Jordan. The State Department man was reasonably fit and appeared to be the most capable.

At the same time he hesitated over whether he should voice his suspicions of Kraske to Jordan. Giving the man a weapon but no warning would be setting him up half-armed. But he didn't want Jordan to inadvertently warn Kraske.

Falcon was hoping that if he gave Kraske enough rope then Kraske would eventually hang himself.

If Kraske didn't succeed first in hanging them all!

In the end the decision was postponed with a new twist in their tortured fortunes. They all heard the fast-approaching roar of the hovercraft returning.

For a moment they were all startled by the noise. Then Gail recognized the sound and gave a joyous shout. She ran to the edge of the lagoon, but Falcon quickly raced after her, caught her and pulled her back.

'Take cover!' he snapped. 'All of you! It may be the SRN5 — but we don't know who might be on board.'

For a split second they gaped at him, then scrambled to obey. Bahadur Rama barked in Nepalese, echoing Falcon and the Gurkhas moved with trained speed. Two of them picked up Sumantri's stretcher, the third lifted Leila bodily, and the baby.

All of them vanished behind the green curtains of vines and foliage. Only Gail still stared uncertainly at the river where it flowed into the forest. Her eyes were uncertain, fear conflicting with hope. Falcon heaved her into cover as the hovercraft burst into the lagoon.

Its arrival shattered the peace and early morning stillness. The birds shrieked and scattered. Spray flew in a wide, pale-green, light-refracting arc as the SRN5 swept close to the far bank and made a tight turn to make a stop in the centre of the lagoon. It faced back downriver and the rotor blades continued to spin, making a bright, whirling disc in the sunlight. It appeared to be ready to accelerate out of the lagoon again as abruptly as it had appeared.

Falcon waited.

Behind him Gail squirmed, uncomfortably and aggressively. His hand on her shoulder kept her pressed firmly down.

Thirty seconds passed. The last bird had flashed out of sight. The muted throb of the hovercraft's engine and the splash of the waterfall were the only sounds. The jungle formed an impenetrable screen for those in hiding.

Then a voice hailed them from the hovercraft.

'Captain Falcon — are you there, sir?'

It was the voice of Tom Harris.

Gail looked up hopefully, but Falcon continued to keep her pinned down. He remained silent and motionless, staring out between the overlapping leaves, and at last she became still.

Falcon could only see Harris at the controls, but that did not necessarily mean the British sergeant was alone. There could easily be a dozen men crouched on the cabin floor below the level of the windows.

Harris called out again. His voice was tense and anxious. And the only certain thing was that Tom Harris was still alive.

Falcon glanced down sternly at Gail, and signed to her to be still. Then he moved silently away from the main party, circling the edge of the lagoon. There was only one way to find out what was happening, but if he drew fire he didn't want any casualties.

When he was well clear he stopped and shouted an answer.

'I'm here, Tom — come on in!'

There was a pause, and then the SRN5 began to move, pulling forward to gain momentum and then turning to push its blunt nose up toward the mud beach. It stopped immediately in front of Falcon the skirt lifted and the craft settled. Harris switched off the engine and the blades revolved slowly to a stop.

The door swung forward, dropping down into the ramp position to touch the beach. Harris appeared in the doorway, looking pale and drawn, one hand holding his submachine gun, the other still in the white sling.

Falcon moved out cautiously into the open.

Bahadur Rama and the three Gurkhas emerged with weapons levelled, just far enough to show that they were there in support.

'Captain Falcon, thank God!' Harris blurted with relief.

He was alone. The hovercraft was empty except for the body of Peter Kennard which was still shrouded in a blanket at the far end of the cabin.

'I don't know who they were,' Harris explained bitterly. 'But they hit us a couple of hours after the rest of you had gone into the jungle to look for the plane crash. I was sitting in the doorway of the hovercraft. The two Gurkhas were on the beach. They'd been poking about around the lagoon — looking for coconuts, I think. The poor little buggers didn't have a chance.'

'How did you escape?'

'Sheer luck, sir. And a bit of help from the Gurkhas. Like I said, I was sitting in the doorway. The sun had moved round and I was getting hot, so I moved back to find the shade. Just as I moved was when we copped the first burst of gunfire. They missed me by half a second and a couple of inches. I ducked into the hovercraft but the Gurkhas got chopped down on the beach.'

Harris paused. His face was sweating and his arm was hurting, but after a moment he went on. 'One of the Gurkhas was killed straight off. The other took a hit in the shoulder but he rolled behind that log we used as a seat. He had guts and I'll give him credit. He held them off while I got the hovercraft started. I yelled at him to come back and he tried, but he didn't make it. The second he moved out of cover he took another hit. There was nothing I could do then but gun the SRN5 and get out of it.'

'How many were in the party that attacked you?'

'I don't know, sir. I didn't see anything of them. It was just bullets flying out of the jungle, and it was all over in a matter seconds.'

'How many weapons were firing? What kind?'

'It sounded like those Russian combat rifles again, sir. Three or four. Maybe more. They were firing so fast it was difficult to tell.'

Falcon frowned. He glanced sideways at Kraske, but Kraske only shrugged. He had no comment to offer. Beside Kraske stood Yamin, his face a bland mask.

'I drove the SRN5 back down the river,' Harris continued. 'But I had to stop at the first rapids. I couldn't control her too well with just one arm. On the open river I was zigzagging all over the bloody place and I knew that over the rapids I'd come to grief. I threw out the anchor and then I tried to think what was best. I finally decided to radio *Scotsman* and see what they advised — and then I found that a bullet had smashed the bloody radio.'

Harris pulled his face into another grimace of bitterness. 'I spent all afternoon trying to fix it, but I didn't have enough of the right spares. I gave up when it got dark, but then it was too late to do anything except stay put for the night. When it got light again I decided that as I couldn't get back downriver the only thing was to take a chance and come back to look for the rest of you.'

'Thank God you did,' Gail said with feeling. 'I don't think Doctor Sumantri or the baby would have survived a three-day trek through the jungle. But now we have the hovercraft back we can get out of this awful place with no more trouble.'

Falcon was not so confident that all their trials were over, but at least the return of the hovercraft had put the odds back in their favour. The lagoon was a dangerous place to linger so he hurried them all on board and left it behind as quickly as possible. Harris was only too glad to relinquish the controls, and most of them felt an almost light-headed sensation of relief as the return journey down the Kiamba began.

There was one thing which the return of Tom Harris proved. The British sergeant no longer fitted the picture as a possible traitor and murderer. Which left all the old questions wide open once more. Falcon plied Harris with more questions in the hope of uncovering clues, but there was nothing Harris could add to his story. He was as bewildered and confused as the rest of them.

But the hovercraft had been attacked with Russian rifles.

Kraske, Yamin and Jusuf would have made three AK-47s.

The armed Dayaks would have made six or more, but Falcon still doubted that they could have used them to such good effect.

Which left the unknown bad guys at Surajong, who could have followed them upriver.

Or perhaps Kraske and his friends were the bad guys from Surajong?

Falcon gave half his mind to mental wrestling with the various possibilities, and the other half to navigation problems and the controls of the SRN5. That was until he had to devote all his concentration to shooting the first stretch of rapids.

The plane passengers who were seeing the hazard for the first time became suddenly silent. Falcon was aware of the hush and the tense, communal indrawing of breath, and he smiled a brief assurance as he steered the hovercraft into the foaming white waters of the ravine.

For the next few minutes they were deafened by the thunder of rushing water. The sheer, slick black walls rose dizzily on either side and the spray boomed upwards in frightening explosions as the river hurtled through the narrow tunnel of rock. The hovercraft swayed wildly from side to side, buffeted by the turbulence and seeming to slide helplessly out of control toward inevitable disaster.

But it wasn't out of control. Falcon's touch was deft and sure on the rudder bar and on the control column. He held back on the power and the sudden swerves were always out of danger and not into a collision. They came out of the broken white maelstrom of the gorge unscathed and the worst was behind them.

The minor rapids which followed caused only a slight quickening of the more nervous heartbeats, and soon they were back to a steady cruising speed on the lower reaches of the river.

Mile after mile the unchanging pattern of the jungle riverbank flowed past on either side, and after three hours they were passing over the wide, shallow loops where they had been ambushed on the outward journey. Falcon gave the hovercraft full speed as they flashed through the danger area, but this time there was nothing to fear. There was no sound of gunfire, and no sign of life on either bank.

Falcon heard Gail's sigh of relief, but Surajong was still ahead.

CHAPTER 14

The town was coming up fast and Falcon ordered them all to lay flat on the floor. The Gurkhas crouched with their submachine guns at the ready, but Falcon was not looking for a fight. He intended to rely upon speed once more and as the river turned a bend and the first shack buildings appeared he gave the stick full forward thrust with the engine at maximum power.

The SRN5 surged forward with a throaty roar, the airspeed indicator needle leaping up quickly to 70 miles per hour. The rickety, stilt-propped huts and the scattered canoes went past in a blur. Faces gaped at them from windows and sagging verandahs, and from along the bamboo wharf, but there was no time for the startled inhabitants to react.

There were half a dozen praus tied up along the waterfront, and two flat-bottomed sampans anchored in midstream. It was the nearest thing to the barricade of boats which Falcon had feared, but there was a gap between the two sampans.

The gap wasn't quite as wide as the hovercraft, but he went through it anyway. He hit both sampans simultaneously, shouldering them aside and forcing the passage. For the hovercraft it was a violent jolt but no more, but for the sampans it was shipwreck and disaster. They were both left sinking fast in the middle of the river.

More huts blurred past, and a fleeting glimpse of the tumbledown mosque, and then the close, green embrace of the jungle enfolded the river once more. They were through, and they had stirred up nothing worse than a frenzied gabble of voices.

It was all too easy. The river began to twist and turn again, but Falcon maintained as much speed as he dared. Moreno and Jordan started to get up to resume their seats, but Falcon glanced back at the first movement and told them curtly to stay down on the floor.

They had raced through Surajong once before, only to find that the ambush had been set just beyond the town. So maybe the bad guys from back there hoped to catch them with the same trick twice.

They did.

But this time it was a trick Falcon couldn't avoid.

The barricade was not one of boats but had been built solid from hundreds of thick bamboo poles and cut logs, and was moored across the whole width of the river. If it had been just a flat raft they could have skimmed over it, but the raft base had been used to mount a four-foot high log fence with a wicked row of sharpened stakes protruding over the top. If they had been travelling upriver the whole construction would have made a superb take-off ramp. Hitting it head-on made a total wreck of the SRN5.

Inevitably it was just behind a sharp, blind bend in the river. Falcon saw it too late and although he tried to throw the hovercraft into reverse they had too much forward momentum. He stamped hard on the rudder bar, veering hard to port in a desperate effort to aim at the more yielding mud and foliage of the riverbank, but there was no time to manoeuvre.

They hit the barricade with a thunderous crash.

From both banks the hidden AK-47s spat bullets which clanged and whined around the armoured hull like a buzz of steel mosquitoes.

The impact threw Falcon forward from his seat and he smashed into the control panel. A glass dial splintered and drew a spurt of blood from the hand he pushed forward to save his face. There were screams and curses from behind him as his companions were catapulted into a struggling heap.

The sharpened ends of the upward-angled stakes had speared through the flexible steel skirting, piercing the plenum chamber and one of the buoyancy tanks. The hovercraft had been spun sideways and started to tilt, but the crash had also knocked loose the barricade from its moorings.

Falcon saw the gap appear between the barrier and the left-hand bank as he pushed himself back into the control seat. The whole ramp-like edifice was swinging slowly open like a huge gate, it was being pushed back by the relentless pressure of the river current.

The hovercraft was settling and within minutes she would be sinking, but while he still had some control Falcon steered her through the gap. He had to get them out from under the AK-47s before they could disembark and desperately he twisted the throttle open and pushed the stick hard forward.

The engine roared and the SRN5 moved sluggishly. The punctured buoyancy tank had half-filled with water and she could no longer get an effective lift. The armoured skirt was dragging in the surface of the river and the craft wallowed as it struggled forward.

Their steel flank scraped against the wooden barricade as they squeezed through. Shouts of anger rose up from both banks and two men in sarongs ran out onto the swinging wooden ramp to blaze away at close range with their rifles.

But Bahadur Rama was on his knees at the window. A sweeping burst from his Sterling scythed across the top of the ramp and both men did a whirling dervish dance of death into the river.

The hovercraft broke clear of the barrier. It was no longer an air-cushion vehicle, but had become a fast-sinking boat. Falcon had no more control but the river current caught them and swept them on their way.

They drifted fast and helpless for a hundred yards before the next bend of the river brought them into a thumping collision with the right-hand bank.

The SRN5 came to rest for the last time, tilting steeply to port as she began to slide under and sink.

'Everybody out!' Falcon yelled to get the stunned diplomats moving, and for the next few minutes they were desperately engaged in the mad scramble to get themselves ashore.

Falcon pushed Sam Jordan out first, and then rapidly handed out Moreno, Gail, Kamala Chavan and Leila Sumantri in swift succession. While Jordan helped to pull them up onto the riverbank, Kraske and Yamin pushed past and jumped ashore.

'Cover us!' Falcon shouted.

Kraske looked back over his shoulder. He raised his rifle as a sign that he had heard, and then plunged into the jungle behind his native ally. Both of them disappeared.

The Gurkhas were struggling with Sumantri's stretcher. Falcon leaped ashore as two of them passed it forward and helped Jordan and Moreno to drag it up the bank. The two Gurkhas followed to assist them.

Bahadur Rama and the last Gurkha were crouched on the sinking chamber platform, taking cover behind the cabin with submachine guns levelled to protect the party from the inevitable attack.

Harris emerged last, white and shaken and still trying to hang on to his submachine gun. He tottered on the edge of the door ramp and almost overbalanced before Gail reached for him and pulled him onto the bank.

Their enemies were running downstream fast from the barricade and shots rang out from the far bank. Bahadur Rama and the soldier beside him gave answering fire, but the hovercraft was disappearing beneath them. Everyone else was on the riverbank and Falcon called to them to abandon the craft.

The two men turned smartly and jumped. The Gurkha sergeant reached the outstretched hand of one of his men and was hauled to safety. The last soldier took two bullets between the shoulder blades and dropped down between the hovercraft and the bank. The river whirled him away and he was lost.

The entire party struggled back from the river's edge, gaining cover from the snipers on the far bank, but they still had the enemy force on their own side to contend with. They heard the crashing of fast approaching bodies coming at them through the undergrowth, rifles crackled and a rain of bullets spattered through the leaves.

Falcon and the surviving Gurkhas formed a thin line, trying to fight a desperate rearguard action as the rest of the party made a stumbling withdrawal along the riverbank. They were hopelessly outnumbered, and hampered by Sumantri's stretcher which Jordan and Moreno carried between them, the retreat was too slow.

The attacking force contained more than a dozen men who were all familiar with the forest and jungle. They spread out quickly to encircle the trapped party, keeping up a non-stop exchange of bullets, and it was only a matter of time before the submachine guns ran out of ammunition.

Gail was helping Leila and Kamala Chavan, steering each of them by an arm as she ran ahead of the stretcher. She was the first to realize they were surrounded and reeled back as a youth with bright black eyes and an AK-47 rifle appeared in front of her.

The youth fired, but in his excitement he missed as Gail ducked and pulled the two women down. Leila screamed and the baby shrieked as he fell momentarily from her arms. Harris was beside them, and holding his Sterling tight against his hip with his elbow he succeeded in triggering an erratic burst with one hand. The youth with the AK-47 was unhurt, but doubled back quickly out of sight.

However, more enemy faces were flitting closer through the trees. They were on three sides now and the non-combatants from the hovercraft threw themselves flat as they were caught in the crossfire.

'MARK!' Gail yelled in panic.

Falcon left the Gurkhas to hold the rear flank and ran to join her, ramming the last magazine into his Sterling as he leaped over the cowering body of Moreno. Behind him Bahadur Rama and his two soldiers fired their last shots, and naked steel flashed in the shafted sunlight as they threw away the Sterlings and drew the curved kukris.

Gail had scooped up the baby and pushed him back into Leila's anguished arms. Then she snatched the Sterling from Harris and crouched beside Falcon. They fired together until both weapons were empty.

The attacking force did not have unlimited ammunition either, and the noise of the battle changed rapidly from the crash of bullets to the sound of shouts and screams and the harsh ring of steel as native parangs clashed with the kukris.

Sam Jordan had picked up the broken branch of a tree and wielded it as a massive club to repel a three-man thrust against the weak centre. All of them who could fight were quickly engaged in scattered hand-to-hand combat.

Falcon swiped the muzzle of his empty Sterling across the teeth of the first man who charged him; dealt the second a cruel kick in the lower belly, and broke the parang-wielding wrist of the third as he flung the man bodily over his shoulder.

He heard Gail scream and whirled to see her carried down into the undergrowth under the weight of two men. He dived after the squirming trio as they rolled toward the riverbank, and hauled her assailants off one at a time. He treated each one to a knuckle-bruising right hook to the jaw that left them both senseless.

For a moment they were clear and he pulled Gail to her feet and glanced round. Harris and two of the Gurkhas were already down, alive or dead he couldn't tell, and he saw Sam Jordan clubbed from behind.

Bahadur Rama was still fighting with tigerish fury. The kukri in his hand no longer gleamed silver but dripped red with blood. But then a parang hacked at his arm and four of his enemies threw themselves on to his back and dragged him down.

Falcon could no longer help any of them. He pulled Gail away and ran her at speed through the tangles of foliage. They lost cover too quickly and skidded to a stop in full sunlight on the very edge of the river.

Like a hunting wolf pack the screams of their enemies were in full cry behind them. Some of them still had a few shots left for more bullets cut through the leaves around their heads.

Falcon decided to risk the crocodiles. He pulled Gail behind him and dived far out into the swirling, dark green flood. The Kiamba swept them away, and in the few seconds it took for their pursuers to reach the riverbank they were gone.

CHAPTER 15

The young man who called himself Commander Mathias was no more than twenty years old. He wore a brown, military-style shirt with strips of red stitched to the epaulettes, and his legs were wrapped loosely in the folds of a dark red sarong. His lank, jet-black hair was tied with a red headband, a badge of authority which was copied by most of his followers. He had the high, broad forehead of an intellectual, but his eyes behind plain, steel-framed spectacles were the hot, wild stare of a fanatic.

'It is unfortunate that your aircraft crashed on the Kiamba.' He addressed the blood-streaked and dishevelled group of his prisoners in high-pitched but understandable English. 'The Kiamba is *my* river! And Surajong is *my* town!'

They were gathered in the dusty, unpaved and refuse-littered square which formed the central meeting place in Surajong. It was a hundred yards back from the river and the main wharf. On three sides it was flanked by dilapidated, colonial style wooden buildings and on the south side by a white-plastered brick building which had once been the police station.

The close knot of captives stood over Sumantri's stretcher which Jordan and Moreno had again been made to carry on a forced march back up the river. Tom Harris was swaying on the point of collapse, his eyes closed and his teeth gritted against the pain from his broken arm. The three Gurkhas had been so badly beaten that they could barely walk, their faces were barely recognizable behind the masks of bloodied cuts and bruises. Leila and Kamala Chavan were near to swooning with exhaustion, and struggling to hold each other up.

All of them were alive, but only just.

Three of the self-termed revolutionary forces were dead, and four more had been badly wounded. It was proof of the fighting ferocity of Bahadur Rama and his two soldiers, and also the reason for the savage battering they had received. If Mathias had not wanted them taken alive they would have been butchered on the spot.

Sam Jordan straightened up from lowering the stretcher and looked slowly round the hostile sea of faces encircling the square. The inner ring consisted of a score of the excited and dangerous young men with the red headbands and rifles. Behind them was the curious flock of native townspeople, most of them women and children, with only a scattering of wrinkled old men.

Jordan looked at his companions and saw that none of them was capable of answering. He was feeling weak and unsteady on his own feet, but he squared his shoulders and faced Mathias to speak for them.

'And just who are you to control this town?'

'I have just told you. I am Commander Mathias — of the Free Kalimantan Revolutionary Forces. I am the Supreme Military Commander of the Kiamba River Region.'

'But how did you get here?'

Mathias smiled, a bitter twist of his thin lips. 'I was born here. And all my comrades were born here. And this is where we saw our fathers die. Here in Surajong — in the great purge when the government murderers hunted down and killed the patriots of the PKI. They were hunted like animals — and those who were not slaughtered endure a living death on Buru and the other political prison islands that are an obscene pox sprinkled across the face of Indonesia. We were children then, and we saw it all — those of us who were not killed with our parents.'

'So maybe you do belong here,' Jordan conceded. 'But you didn't find Kalashnikov rifles growing on the trees.'

'We have friends outside Indonesia. Many friends. Some of my comrades here have been trained at the PLO training camp at Hamouriya in Syria. The Palestinians are our friends. The Syrians and the Libyans are our friends. I myself have attended the Patrice Lumumba University in Moscow. There I have studied Marxist philosophy, the organization of the Soviet Communist Party, and the international class struggle. The USSR is our very, very good friend.'

'And no doubt you had a bit of extra schooling from the GRU,' Jordan observed sourly.

Mathias looked surprised. 'You are correct. How did you guess?'

'It's common knowledge,' Jordan retorted. 'Military instruction for terrorists inside Russia is the responsibility of the Third Department of Soviet Military Intelligence — under the overall supervision of the KGB, of course.'

Mathias shrugged. 'The USSR is our Number One friend,' he repeated.

'What do you mean to do with us?' Moreno asked the question, his voice shaking a little with apprehension. 'Why have you brought us here?'

Mathias looked at him with contempt. 'There are many reasons. One is that you are all enemies of the continuing World Revolution. It began with Marx and Lenin in the USSR, and it will not end until you and all the decadent bloodsuckers who are allied to the West have been destroyed. America, the Great Satan of the West!' He screamed at Jordan. 'Will be destroyed!'

The rebel youths cheered and made the clenched fist salute. It was not a moment to interrupt and Jordan bit his lip and said nothing.

However, they were learning quickly that Mathias tended to speak in short bursts of violent rhetoric. This one was over, and after smiling for a moment he turned his gaze back to Moreno to continue almost calmly.

'There is another reason. Now that you are here I simply cannot let you go.'

'Why not?' Kamala Chavan had recovered her breath and spoke up with an effort at dignity. 'Senor Moreno, Mister Jordan, Doctor Sumantri and myself, all represent our countries at the United Nations. Our joint mission is one of peace — to bring justice and stability, and political co-existence to South East Asia, without all this foolishness of terrorism, and killing, and destruction.'

'Shut up old grandmother,' Mathias sneered at her. 'You are more stupid than you are senile. And you know nothing. You should be at home, wiping the noses of your children's children — not interfering in the world of men.'

It was a taunt the Indian woman had heard often before, and she had long ago devised a scathing retort. It was one she was careful not to use when facing a microphone or a TV camera, but it had proved very useful in crushing hecklers at small town or village level rallies.

'If I am senile and stupid,' she declared, 'then you have not even been born yet. Politically you are still the sperm in your father's penis.'

There was a stunned silence. From the back of the crowd there came a few girlish titters of laughter. Commander Mathias raised a clenched fist and trembled with fury. Some of his men were grinning slowly. He had been made to look a fool and spittle frothed over his lower lip.

Jordan stepped quickly between them and pushed the grey-haired woman back behind Leila and Moreno. 'That's enough, Kamala,' he warned her quickly. 'This isn't an election campaign with a squad of policemen to step in if it gets too rough.'

'But where are the police?' Sumantri spoke weakly from his stretcher. 'Kalimantan is administered by the Indonesian government. There should be a government representative.'

'Yes.' Moreno glanced hopefully to the sun-bleached and paint-flaking sign over the police building. 'Where are the police? There must be some real authority here.'

Mathias laughed, the blind humour of the idea helping to appease his ruffled dignity. He translated for those of his followers who did not understand, and they all expressed various levels of glee. Two of the revolutionaries hurried into the police station and dragged out a terrified little fat man in a khaki shirt and shorts.

'Meet Inspector Darmo,' Mathias said scornfully. 'Unfortunately he no longer has any policemen to command. They have both seen the wisdom of joining the Revolutionary Forces. We keep the inspector alive because he has learned to do as he is told — and he is a useful figurehead on the rare occasions when we receive any interest from Djakarta.'

He made a sign and the unhappy little fat man was bundled back inside the police station. Kicks and cat-calls chased him on his way.

Clearly there was no effective government authority at Surajong. Mathias and his men had total control of the whole town.

'Just what do you hope to achieve?' Jordan asked. 'What's the purpose of all this? Do you really think you can set up your own little kingdom here on the Kiamba?'

'Not my kingdom,' Mathias insisted. 'We are just a small part of the international class struggle and World Revolution. Surajong is our base and we will begin with the liberation of all Kalimantan. We are arming and training the Dayak tribesmen of the interior, and when we are ready we will lead them to attack Sarawak and Sabah. In Brunei we have links with student revolutionaries who have been trained in Libya. As soon as the last British forces and their despicable Nepalese mercenary troops have been withdrawn, the new revolutionary forces will unite to achieve total victory.'

'And after Borneo, the rest of Indonesia,' Jordan guessed shrewdly.

'But of course.' Mathias was in the full swing of his rhetoric once again and was playing to the crowd. 'Borneo is just the beginning, and all the Indonesian islands will be just stepping stones to Djakarta. The Indonesian Communist Party will be reborn again. Our fathers were massacred in their thousands, but the Muslim capitalists and traitors did not kill all of the children. A new generation is growing up to swell the ranks of a new PKI. But now we have been trained in new military techniques, and new political ideals. And this time we have revenge for our fathers to spur us on to our goal.'

'You'll still fail,' Jordan told him bluntly. 'The whole thing is starting to fall apart right now — because this secret base of yours isn't going to be secret for much longer. Maybe you haven't noticed, but the rains have stopped. The weather has cleared to the north. Any time now there's gonna be an air search made to find our crashed plane.'

Mathias twisted his mouth into an angry scowl. 'This is a difficulty. I was not responsible for the crash of your aircraft, and it has caused much trouble for me. I am not ready yet for the outside world to know that my forces control the river.'

'Who was responsible for the crash?' Jordan asked quickly.

Mathias shrugged. 'I do not know. Friends of the Revolution who knew you were fit only to die, but who did not know of our presence here on the Kiamba. Or who did not intend your aeroplane to crash in this area. It was an unfortunate mistake.'

'Too bad.' Jordan taunted the other man to keep him talking.

'Not so bad that we cannot put it right,' Mathias snarled. 'We received a radio warning from Kuching to say that the hovercraft was on its way. Unfortunately I was down the river at Batakan when the message came through. My deputy commander tried to stop the hovercraft with our heavy machine guns — and he was killed with some of my best men. For this, and for your other crimes, you will all pay.'

'You cannot kill us,' Luis Moreno protested. 'The authorities will find out. You will pay in your turn.'

'But I do not intend to kill you.' Mathias smiled thinly and behind his spectacles his eyes gleamed with sadistic humour. 'We shall simply take you back up the river and return you to the Dayaks. They knew you were important and believed that I wanted you alive, but this time I shall ensure they understand that they can take *all* the heads. If your crashed plane is ever found again, then all your bodies and the bodies of the hovercraft crew will be scattered around the wreckage. It will appear as though the Dayaks are wholly responsible.'

Leila Sumantri stared at him, and silently fainted.

Jordan's throat was dry. 'The hovercraft,' he said hoarsely. 'How are you gonna explain away the bullet holes in the hovercraft?'

Mathias shrugged. 'The hovercraft can be towed into a side creek and sunk without trace. It will be a jungle mystery, never to be solved.'

Sam Jordan had no more questions.

It was hot in the square. The sun was a white blaze of heat burning directly over their heads, and the self-styled Commander Mathias had at last tired of boasting and parading to the crowd. He made a brief speech in the local dialect and the prisoners were laughed at, spat upon, and dragged roughly away.

'You can share a police cell with the good Inspector Darmo,' he called after them. 'And we can find another cell for your Nepalese mercenaries.'

The two groups were separated and the Gurkhas subjected to the worst of the violence and the abuse. Most of the Kiamba revolutionaries who had died had fallen victims to the wicked, curved kukris, and now Bahadur Rama and his two surviving soldiers had to grit their teeth and take their punishment.

Mathias watched with approval, and then turned to hurl a final taunt at the UN peace mission.

'We know that one man and a woman escaped into the river. Probably they have been devoured by the crocodiles, but if they have not then my men will soon find them. As soon as we have hunted them down — or as soon as we are sure they are dead — we will begin the journey back up the river to reunite you all with the headhunters.'

CHAPTER 16

Mathias had groups of men searching the riverbanks on either side below the point where the hovercraft had come to grief, but they were all wasting their time. Falcon had left the river after it had carried him round the first bend, and already he had mapped out his continuing battle plan.

They emerged from the swift, muddy waters only yards ahead of the first hungry crocodile, and Falcon had to clamp his hand hard over Gail's mouth to stop her from screaming as the cheated jaws snapped at their heels. Ruthlessly, but silently, he had dragged her away from the river's edge, pushing deep into the jungle before they could again attract any pursuit.

When he had calmed Gail and she had recovered from her fright they moved north, giving the river a wide berth but following its course back upstream. They circled the combat zone where the terrorists were gathering up their prisoners, and as soon as he dared Falcon moved back to the riverbank to find the wide path leading back to Surajong.

They moved fast, even though Gail was panting and struggling to keep up. Behind them Mathias and his men were burdened with half-crippled and unwilling prisoners, who were in turn burdened with Sumantri's stretcher, so it proved an easy race for Falcon to win. Even so he calculated the risk that Mathias might send runners ahead to announce his victory, so he kept up a cracking pace.

They reached the township with a good half mile lead. Enough time to make another detour through the jungle and reach a grove of coconut palms on the north side before Mathias and his triumphant procession entered from the south.

The noise and excitement had drained the town as its inhabitants flocked to congregate around the central square. It gave Falcon the opportunity he needed to make his final run through the empty back alleys to reach the crumbling sanctuary of the broken-down Muslim mosque. They ducked into the courtyard where Gail sank down gasping against the wall.

Falcon looked round with satisfaction at the obvious signs of abandonment. The courtyard was littered with rubbish, and the pool was only half filled with stagnant water. Huge chunks of plaster had broken from the walls which were paint-daubed with hostile graffiti. Most of the mosaic tiles had been ripped from the dome and doorway of the mosque, and one of the two minaret towers had been completely demolished.

'Come on.' He pulled Gail to her feet and led her over to the slender tower which was still standing. It was cool in the gloomy interior and he led her quickly up the steep, winding stairway to the top. They emerged into blinding sunlight again on the tiny cupola platform where the *imam* would once have called the faithful to prayer.

They knelt behind the low, protecting wall, and from here they had a high view over the whole town. Gail was unimpressed and collapsed into a slumped heap. Her chest was heaving, her heart was pounding, and she was blinded by her own sweat in her eyes.

'This is crazy,' she said at last, when she could speak. 'We can't stay here. They must find us.'

'Maybe we'll get lucky,' Falcon murmured calmly. 'This whole town has been taken over by communist-inspired terrorists. To gain complete control they must have driven out the Muslims, or terrorized them into keeping a low profile. This mosque has not been used for a long time. No one comes here anymore. Except perhaps children to climb on the walls and play. I think they will be our only risk.'

Gail was silent for another minute. Then she raised her head and joined him in looking out over the town. Below them was an untidy jumble of palm thatch and rusted corrugated tin roofs. Over to their right the sun glittered on the sweeping curve of the river, and directly ahead, perhaps 150 yards away, was the packed town square.

'What's happening?' Gail asked.

'The top cat among the bad guys is reading the riot act,' Falcon answered. 'He's the one with the red headband and the glasses who is doing most of the arm-waving and talking. It looks like Jordan is speaking up and giving him some back, but there's so much chatter in the background that I can't make out much of what they are saying.'

Gail squinted her eyes, using her hand to shield them from the bright glare of the sun. She was trying to pick out the individual faces.

'I can't see any sign of Steve Kraske.'

'Kraske isn't there. His Javanese buddy isn't there either.'

'So maybe they escaped too. If we could join up with them?'

'Maybe he got away,' Falcon agreed. 'But somehow I don't think we can rely on much help from Mister Kraske. He disappeared pretty damn smart on the riverbank.'

'He could have been killed.' Falcon had not shared his doubts with her and Gail was surprised by the sourness of his tone. 'Or maybe he saw that it was hopeless and broke away, the same as you had to in the finish.'

Falcon did not argue. He was trying to overhear the broken snatches of dialogue that filtered up from the square.

Gail remained silent until they saw the prisoners dragged away and lost from their view, and the crowd began to disperse. Then she spoke again in a dull voice which showed she considered their position to be hopeless.

'Mark, what are we going to do?'

'Wait until nightfall,' Falcon said calmly. 'There are half a dozen useful looking boats moored up along the waterfront, and there are plenty of automatic weapons floating around this town with only inexperienced kids in charge of them. Give me the cover of darkness and the chance to create some confusion — and maybe we can start pulling some of our chestnuts back out of the fire.'

Throughout the long, hot hours of the afternoon Falcon watched and waited. The diplomats had been taken into the old police building and did not reappear. The Gurkhas were removed to one of three more solid brick and timber buildings on the south edge of the town. The buildings had the appearance of an old army barracks flanking a small parade ground with an old flagpole, and Falcon guessed that it had probably been used to house Indonesian troops during their war with Malaysia. Now it had been taken over by the bulk of the terrorist forces. There would be a guardhouse, Falcon reasoned, and that had to be where the Gurkhas would be imprisoned. Obviously there had not been room for all the prisoners in the cells at the police station.

There was only one other brick building in the whole ramshackle township. It was down on the wharf at the corner of the main road which ran up to the north side of the square. It looked as though it had once housed the customs or whatever other government authority the town had possessed, but now it had been taken over as the terrorist HQ. Or, to be more precise, it served as the private living quarters of the man who called himself Commander Mathias.

The rest of Surajong was just a maze of stinking mud alleys.

Falcon had eight hours before darkness in which to memorize every detail of the layout.

Eight hours in which to watch every move of Mathias and the strutting young lords with their AK-47s and red communist headbands.

And eight hours in which to plan his own moves with infinite care.

He knew that once he made his first move there would be no time for any further planning. He would have to hit hard and fast and keep moving. He would have to play the role of a small army, using every commando tactic he knew to turn Surajong into a town of blind, helpless panic and confusion.

It was a tall order for any one man — but if any man could do it then that man was Mark Falcon.

The groups of men Mathias had detailed to search the riverbanks began returning to the town to report their failure in the late afternoon and evening. By sunset the terrorist strength in Surajong had almost doubled, a fact which filled Gail with more despair. Falcon was undeterred. If he had judged the situation right there was only one leader. Remove Mathias and it would not matter how many headless chickens there might be to run circles in the havoc he intended to create.

The sun died in flares of gold and crimson above the palm groves and jungle treetops to the east. And then they got lucky. Black clouds blotted out the stars and a series of monsoon thunderstorms poured deluge after deluge over the rooftops, driving the populace indoors.

Falcon waited for the dead hours of early morning, and for another downpour to give him total cover. Then with Gail moving reluctantly at his heels they left the shelter of the mosque.

The rain hit them with stinging force, blinding them and deafening them as it rattled violently on the corrugated tin of the rooftops. Gail cried out in fear and anguish, an involuntary yelp that was quickly smothered in the noise of the storm.

She was lost and helpless, but Falcon's grip was steel-fingered on her wrist and she stumbled after him through the mud alley as he ran swiftly for the coconut grove. From there he skirted the edge of the town, trusting to his instinct, his memory, and his natural sense of direction to bring them round to the barracks.

When they arrived he left Gail on the edge of the jungle, ordering her not to move until he came back. She stayed, shivering and terrified, listening to the rain drumming through the foliage behind her. Falcon had been instantly swallowed up by the pouring darkness and she wondered how he would ever find her again.

Alone Falcon could move faster, and the rain gave him all the cover he needed. From his observations during the day he knew that the long wooden building on the east side of the square provided the main living quarters for the terrorists. The Gurkhas had been taken into the identical building on the opposite side of the parade ground, so obviously that incorporated the guardhouse. The third building, a smaller, brick-built structure at the south end of the parade ground would have once been the administration block. He had watched several terrorists go inside and emerge fitting full magazines to the combat rifles, which meant it must now house their armoury. All his targets were pinpointed.

He had decided to release the Gurkhas first.

There were just two guards in the east-side building and they were both asleep on their sagging rope and timber beds. The door was unlocked and Falcon did not even have to kill them. Two swift, accurate chopping blows from the hard edge of his palm ensured that they would stay asleep for some considerable time.

Falcon collected up the two AK-47s propped against the wall, and the large ring of keys which hung at the belt of one of the guards. The solid, hardwood door to the guardhouse was at the far end of the building. Falcon unlocked it and it creaked open. The wide awake eyes of Bahadur Rama gleamed at him faintly in the darkness.

'Morning, Sergeant,' Falcon said softly. 'Feeling fit enough for some action?'

'Captain Falcon, sah.' Bahadur Rama returned the whisper joyfully. Then he lied. 'All okay, sah.'

Falcon knew the Gurkha had a bloodied bandage round the deep wound on his upper arm, but he guessed Bahadur Rama could still use a rifle. He passed over one of the AK-47s and together they woke the two Gurkha soldiers.

Falcon led them outside. The rain still thundered out of the blackness and with no fear of discovery he led them to the administration block. There were no guards and the room which served as the armoury was wide open. The young terrorists were so convinced of their own prowess and invincibility that they had not bothered to take even the most basic precautions.

Falcon quickly found two more rifles for the two Gurkha soldiers, and spare magazines for all of them. Much to their joy he also located the three kukri knives that had been taken away from them.

He armed himself with two additional rifles and six Russian-made hand grenades. He found string bags of the type worn by the Viet Cong and filled two of them with three grenades each, which he tied on to his belt.

Satisfied that he had as much explosive and firepower as he could comfortably carry he led them out and back to the edge of the jungle where Gail waited. She almost sobbed with relief at his return.

At this stage Falcon had no time for emotional reunions. Instead he quickly briefed the Gurkhas.

'Take your men down to the river,' he told Bahadur Rama. 'And take Doctor Crawford with you. There are several native praus tied up along the waterfront. Find the one with the most powerful auxiliary engine and bring it to the south end of the wharf. I'll send Jordan and the others there to meet you.'

'Yes, sah.' Bahadur Rama nodded grimly to show that he understood.

'One more thing,' Falcon concluded. 'If you have to kill anyone, do it silently. There'll be plenty of noise and diversions, but we don't want any attention drawn to the wharf.'

Bahadur Rama smiled and drew out the kukri which only minutes before he had returned to its scabbard. 'Quietly, sah,' he promised. 'Very quietly.'

Falcon turned to Gail. 'When they select a boat you get on board and stay there. Keep your head down.'

'Mark—' Her eyes were full of anguished questions, but then she swallowed them back and nodded. 'Yes, Mark.'

Falcon kissed her, handed her over to the Gurkhas, and sent them on their way.

He headed fast for his next target, the police building on the edge of the central square. It was a small town and he was there within two minutes. He slowed up to reconnoitre with care, and give the Gurkhas time to do their job.

He circled the building. There was only one door, facing the square, and the cell windows at the back of the building were all barred. With his shoulders flat against the wall he risked a one-eye survey through the only window that did not have bars. It was at the front of the building and looked into a lighted room where three terrorist guards sat at a table. They were all wide awake, smoking cigarettes and playing cards.

In the same moment Falcon became aware of the hushed silence. The background drumming of the rain had stopped, and now there was only a faint dripping from the wet rooftops.

His cover had gone.

Well, he couldn't expect to be lucky all of the time. And it was too much to hope that all the guards would be asleep.

He waited five minutes, giving Bahadur Rama plenty of time, and then he kicked open the door and went in.

One of the terrorists was looking directly at the door. He opened his mouth and gave a wild yell of alarm. All of them were young and foolish. They ignored Falcon's snapped command to be still and dived for their weapons.

The first youth died while he was still only halfway up from his chair, the burst from Falcon's AK-47 smashing into his shoulder and the wall of his chest. The second was cut down while his hands were still a yard from his weapon. The third actually got his hands on to the AK-47 leaning against the wall behind him, but Falcon's continuing burst hammered him into a crumpled heap before he could use it.

The violence of the gunfire had at last shattered the sleeping stillness of the night. The table had been overturned and the oil lamp which had lighted the card game had smashed on the floor. Bright flames spread and licked quickly upwards.

Falcon didn't waste time in hunting for the keys. He simply shot the locks off the two cell doors where the diplomats were secured, and threw one of the spare rifles into the startled hands of Sam Jordan.

'Get them moving,' he commanded. 'There's an alley to your right as you go out the door. It'll take you down to the wharf. The Gurkhas will be there with a boat.'

Jordan was momentarily bewildered. 'What — how — what about you?'

'I'll join you in a few minutes. Right now I've got to cover your back. So move it!'

He whirled and was gone.

The self-styled Commander Mathias was snoring gently when the harsh crackle of automatic rifle fire disturbed his peace. He sat up abruptly, spat curses in Javanese and Russian, and grabbed in the darkness for his pants and spectacles.

The girl who had been sleeping with him was also rudely awakened. He had used her to his total satisfaction and her sweat-slippery naked body was still entangled with his own. He struggled free from her, swearing at her to shut her up. Her babbling questions were a hindrance to his efforts to act and think.

If he had stayed with her he might have lived. Instead he ran out onto the verandah just as Falcon arrived after a lightning sprint from the police building.

He saw bright red muzzle flashes and felt the bullets ripping into his chest and stomach. He was crucified in his own doorway, the impact flinging him back with his arms spread wide. His weapon fell clattering from his hand and the red juices spilled out of him.

The impossible had happened, and he died wondering why.

A window smashed in the same moment, and a hand grenade exploded inside the house. The crack of flame found more combustible materials and the interior of the house began to burn fiercely.

The girl ran screaming, still naked, from the back of the building.

Falcon was already doubling back to the police building, doing everything now on the run as he weaved through the muddy alleyways. He saw the tail end of Jordan's little column disappearing toward the river, and tossed another of his grenades into the now empty police building to add to the confusion.

The disturbed townspeople were beginning to spill into the central square. Falcon emptied his AK-47 over their heads and threw it away. He unslung one of the fully-loaded weapons from his shoulder and raced on toward the barracks.

The first wave of Syrian-trained terrorists had rubbed the sleep out of their eyes, grabbed their trousers and guns, and were charging toward the centre of the town. Falcon bowled a hand grenade to meet them and blasted two of them into the air. The others scattered with cries of panic as he ripped off another burst of rifle fire.

Without stopping he ducked into a side alley, sped on for a hundred yards, took the next right for fifty and then the next right again. He was behind the demoralized first wave when he emptied the magazine into their tails.

He spun round before the answering bullets could find him, zigzagging at speed until he reached the barracks. The second wave of terrorists was emerging and he flipped a grenade into their startled ranks. As they milled in helpless, screaming confusion in the aftermath of the explosion he dodged behind their sleeping block.

He had saved the last hand grenade for a return visit to the armoury. He tossed it through the window and blew the entire administration building sky-high in a spectacular chain of explosions.

By now he had done a pretty good job of creating hell, fire and havoc. And any terrorist strength that was left was being drawn to the back of the town and the barracks.

It was time to duck out of sight and keep a low profile as he hurried down to the river.

Sam Jordan had followed the back alley down to the mudbank of the river, and stood there uncertainly, holding the AK-47 in his hands. Behind him Moreno was trembling at the head of the stretcher. Harris and Leila had struggled with the rear handles, while Kamala Chavan carried the baby.

Further back the whole town was now an uproar of shouting voices, screams, shots, explosions and flames. Jordan bit his lip, wondering where in hell to move next, and then Bahadur Rama's whisper reached him from the shadows.

'Here, sah. This way.'

They turned to duck under the raised floor of one of the stilt-propped riverside houses, their feet slipping on mud, filth and refuse. The stink as they bent low was appalling, but it only lasted for a few minutes.

They emerged onto the end of the wooden wharf and the Gurkha sergeant led them to the waiting boat. Gail and the two soldiers reached up willing hands to take the stretcher.

Jordan was the last to go on board, and as he did so a rush of feet sounded along the wharf. Jordan spun round, raising his rifle, then lowering it again as he recognized the familiar red-headed American.

'Steve,' Gail said thankfully, and then her voice wavered as she realized that he was pointing an AK-47 between her eyes.

'Kraske!' Falcon called sharply.

Kraske turned to look over his shoulder and saw the tall, grim-faced, combat-ready figure of the Falcon moving out onto the wharf behind him.

For a second Kraske hesitated, undecided. His face was struggling to find the right expression. Then he lowered the rifle, forcing himself to relax.

'Mark, thank God. I knew it had to be you. Mathias recognized me and held me separate from the others. I guess he had some special kind of interrogation in mind for me.'

He paused, swallowing hard, his face sweating. 'Luckily I managed to get away when you started all this ruckus. I figured you had to be aiming for a boat to get downriver. So I ran to join you.'

Falcon stared at him. There wasn't a second to waste and somehow he couldn't just shoot Kraske down in cold blood.

'Get on board,' he ordered.

Kraske grinned, slung his rifle over one shoulder and jumped into the prau. Falcon followed him.

Bahadur Rama cast off as one of the Gurkhas started the engine.

The sudden roar brought their enemies rushing down to the river, but they had sped almost out of sight round the first bend before the first fusillade of shots cracked over their wake.

They left Surajong burning, a chaotic, trampled ant heap writhing in flames.

CHAPTER 17

The prau turned the blind bend in the river and in the faint starlight they saw the black shadow of the massive ramp barricade that had wrecked the SRN5. It still hung like an open gate from its right-hand moorings. Falcon ordered Bahadur Rama to shut down the auxiliary engine and bring the native boat to a stop against the right-hand bank, close behind the breached barrier.

The Gurkha sergeant obeyed without question, and Falcon quickly threw out the heavy rock which was tied on to a length of rope and served as the boat's anchor. The others stared at him in bewilderment. Their hearts were still racing and most of them hadn't yet recovered from the shock of their desperate escape from Surajong.

'Sergeant,' Falcon said grimly. 'How many boats as big and fast as this one did we leave behind?'

'I think two, Sah, with same big engine.'

'So we can expect some hot pursuit,' Falcon explained to the rest of them. 'Just as soon as those young hotheads get organized and find a new leader. And maybe one of those boats will have a faster engine than ours. Or we could be the first to run out of gas.'

'So let us get the hell out of here!' Kraske urged.

'No.' Falcon said flatly. 'I'm getting sour at being the target of every goddamned ambush on the Kiamba. It's about time we played these guys at their own game. I'm going to sink those two boats as they come round the bend. Then if we do meet up with any more trouble downstream — then at least we'll know we're not going to have another couple of boatloads of terrorists piling up on our backs.'

'It makes sense,' Sam Jordan said slowly.

'Sure it does. We have five rifles. Six with yours, Sam. If you want in?'

Jordan looked down at the weapon in his hands, then back at Falcon 'I'm a politician, Mark — on a peace mission. But I'm getting damn tired of being pushed around. I reckon I'm in.'

'Good. So let's move into position.'

They climbed ashore, Falcon, the three Gurkhas, Kraske and then Jordan. In single file Falcon led them back up the riverbank path, past the trailing barrier.

Kraske stopped.

'I'll drop off here, Mark. I'll cover your rear flank.'

Falcon turned to face him. Kraske's craggy features were shadowed innocence in the gloom. Falcon sensed a warning look and an imperceptible negative shake of the head from Bahadur Rama, but he pretended not to notice.

'Okay,' he told Kraske. 'You have the rear flank.'

He moved on, posting one of the Gurkhas, then Jordan, the second Gurkha, and finally Bahadur Rama. He set them in a line, roughly ten feet apart, with instructions to clear themselves a field of fire through the foliage overhanging the river.

He paused before leaving Bahadur Rama.

'You have the front flank, Sergeant,' he stressed carefully. 'If possible let both praus get round the bend before you open fire, but don't let the first one get past the barrier.'

The Gurkha sergeant stared at him for a moment, and then he glimpsed the meaning behind the first five words. His teeth gleamed approval and he nodded his full understanding.

Falcon moved a little further up the river, and there he waited for five minutes before he backed off silently into the jungle. Frogs croaked noisily, the night insects droned, and further back in the forest there were faint, nocturnal rustlings that might have been no more than a breath of air through the leaves. Falcon made no sound that could be heard above these, and even Bahadur Rama did not realize that he was moving stealthily down river behind the ambush line.

When he judged that he was directly behind Kraske, Falcon froze. Two minutes later Kraske shifted slightly to ease a cramped limb, and the movement was only a few yards to the left of where Falcon had expected it to be. Inch by inch he eased forward, closing the gap between them.

He saw Kraske's silhouette in the gloom. Kraske was not watching the river. Instead he was facing up the path. He had the trusted position he had aimed for over the past two days, the rearguard point where he could cover the whole line. He held his AK-47 ready to fire, and his head was cocked slightly to one side as he listened for the first sound of the pursuit boats from Surajong.

Falcon called softly from the darkness.

'*Stefan.*'

'*Da.*'

In the moment of tension Kraske had slipped, answering the Russian equivalent of his name with the Russian affirmative. In the same split second he realized that he had been trapped and spun on his heel.

'*Don't.*' Falcon warned him. 'Drop the rifle.'

Kraske swore. He knew he was only a hair-trigger from death and quickly he dropped the rifle. Then slowly he completed the turn.

'So Steve is Stefan,' Falcon said grimly. 'And Kraske is Kraskovitich

— or Kraskonov — or is it just plain Kraski?'

Kraske hesitated, and then at last he shrugged. 'I guess I knew I wasn't really fooling you, Mark. How long have you been certain?'

'Almost from the beginning. You talked about the USSR — the full, glorified title — when a real American would have just said Russia or the Soviet Union. Then you made another mistake when you were talking to Jordan. I didn't catch on right away because it was Gail who tripped you, and I was wishing she hadn't interfered. You told her that when you lived off the jungle with Yamin and his group in the early sixties you all ate wild pig. But earlier you had told us that Yamin and his group were all anti-communist Muslims — and Muslims don't eat pork.'

'You are too clever, Mark,' Kraske complimented him bitterly.

'Smart enough to add two and two,' Falcon agreed. 'And there was only one way it could add up. Either you had to be what you said you were, a CIA agent who had worked with anti-communist guerrillas. Or you had to be the opposite — a KBG agent who had worked with pro-communist guerrillas. And still working with the terrorists.'

Kraske tightened his mouth and said nothing.

'I guess Yamin and Jusuf were old friends,' Falcon continued. 'But Commander Mathias was your new protégé. Maybe you were on that other river when the hovercraft came up the Kiamba, otherwise the first ambush might have been better planned. But you had to follow us, and it was either you or one of your two colleagues who killed Peter Kennard. Later you shot down the two Gurkha soldiers at the lagoon, but unluckily for you Tom Harris got away with the SRN5.'

Kraske swallowed nervously. He was still admitting nothing, but he couldn't help glancing sideways and hoping that Bahadur Rama and the two surviving soldiers were not listening.

'You followed us out to the crash site,' Falcon went on. 'But the odds were still against you for a straight fight. So you played the CIA man, and hoped to take us from the inside when the time was ripe. I figure too that Mathias must have suborned the Dayaks and set them up with modern weapons. You didn't have any direct links there. The Dayaks didn't know your face. So for a little while we were on the same side. You didn't want to lose your head any more than any of us.'

'They killed my good friend Jusuf,' Kraske reminded him.

'And what about Corporal Ganju?' Falcon asked. 'Did the Dayaks kill him? Or did Yamin kill him just because an opportunity arose to bring down the odds a little further?'

Kraske licked his dry lips, and then said slowly. 'We left our radio hidden close by the lagoon. Yamin slipped away from the camp during the night to put a report back to Surajong. The Gurkha followed. He must have been suspicious. Yamin had to kill him.'

It was Kraske's first admission of guilt. The first crack in his wall of silence. Falcon watched him carefully and tried another question.

'When we were in the Dayak longhouse you shot a headhunter out of the rafters when he was aiming a poisoned dart at me. I figure you meant to put that bullet in my back — but you changed your mind. Why?'

'Because the Gurkhas came through the longhouse too damned fast. That sergeant of yours was looking me right in the eye.' He paused and licked his lips again. 'That's a good man, Mark. He had his doubts about me too. Every time I thought you might be about to turn your back on me — that Gurkha sergeant was looking at me over the barrel of his goddamn submachine gun.'

Falcon began to read Kraske's mind. The Russian was afraid of Bahadur Rama and the two Gurkhas. He was loosening up, giving out a little information, so that Falcon would have a reason to protect him and keep him alive.

'You were not a prisoner at Surajong,' Falcon concluded. 'You were an honoured guest. You just kept out of sight because you didn't know whether I might appear again, and whether your CIA cover story might still prove useful.'

Kraske nodded. 'I figured you were not dumb enough to drown, Mark. And the crocs would have found you too tough a mouthful.'

'So you waited for me to make my move. Then you got smart and headed for the wharf to cut us off. You were never running to join us — you meant to stop our escape.'

Kraske nodded. 'But you came up behind me. You had the drop on me. That's why I had to switch back to my cover role. Except that I need not have bothered. You had it all worked out, Mark. You knew back there on the wharf.'

He paused hopefully. 'You knew, Mark, but you couldn't kill me in cold blood. You're a killer in action — but not cold. You couldn't gun me down on the wharf, and you can't do it now.'

'Don't bet on it,' Falcon warned him grimly.

They faced each other for another moment, and then they both heard the sound of boat engines coming down the Kiamba. The boats were approaching fast, the first faint whine swelling quickly into a speeding roar.

'Turn around!' Falcon snapped. 'Face the river!'

Kraske hesitated, but he knew he didn't have one chance in a thousand. He hunched up his shoulders and winced in anticipation as he turned to face the river.

Falcon slugged him hard behind the left ear with the butt of the AK-47.

When the two native praus hurtled fast around the blind bend in the river, Falcon was not in the least bit surprised to see the familiar face of Yamin in command of the leading craft. Starlight showed up the stony features, and glinted on the automatic weapon in his hands.

Both boats were packed with terrorists in red headbands, all of them armed to the teeth and hell-bent on vengeance.

And hell came halfway to meet them.

Falcon had moved out onto the raft barricade, crouching on one knee with his own rifle at the ready and Kraske's weapon laid close within reach. He and Bahadur Rama opened fire simultaneously when the terrorists were between them, catching both praus in a vicious crossfire. A split second later Jordan and the two Gurkha soldiers were adding more bullets to the slaughter.

Falcon killed Yamin with his first burst, blasting the Javanese backward into the river with no regrets. It evened the score for Corporal Ganju. The man at the tiller was his second target and the terrorist spun sideways, dragging the tiller hard over as he went.

The prau slammed bow first into the raft barrier and its rough-hewn planks and timbers fell apart. The single mast snapped at deck level and scythed two terrorists over the side, and the rest floundered helplessly as the wreckage sank beneath them.

Two of the terrorists tried to return Falcon's fire. Both were quickly cut down for their pains. The others found themselves swimming for their lives. Those who tried to reach the near bank were driven back by more short bursts of fire.

Falcon drove them over to the far bank, where without their weapons they could do no harm.

The second prau had swerved away from the ambush and rammed the far bank. There it was shot to pieces below the waterline by Jordan and the three Gurkhas. The young terrorists spilled out of it, shouting and screaming as the river current sucked it down.

There were ominous splashes along both riverbanks as the crocodiles scented blood and made their slithering nosedives into the churning water.

Falcon shouted the order to cease fire.

The Gurkhas and Jordan came back to meet him on the footpath. They picked up the unconscious Kraske and slung him into the waiting prau. Gail and the baffled diplomats viewed the proceedings with total incomprehension.

Bahadur Rama started the engine and Falcon took the tiller. One of the Gurkhas pulled in the anchor rock and they continued their interrupted journey down the river.

CHAPTER 18

It was daylight when Kraske slowly blinked open his eyes. The fierce flashes of sunlight stabbed painfully through the overhanging foliage, and his head ached as though the back of his neck had been run over by a tank. He was lying on his side on the thick bamboo matting which formed the deck of the prau, and his wrists were tied behind his back.

When he twisted his head he saw Bahadur Rama staring at him with cold, hostile eyes. The Gurkha squatted only a yard away with his rifle across his knees. He did not speak or smile, but his right hand strayed hopefully so that the fingers could caress the black hardwood hilt of the kukri in its scabbard at his hip.

Kraske swallowed on a dry throat and tried to suppress a shiver.

The prau was moving silently without engine power. The river current was fast after the rains, and Falcon was using it to conserve petrol which they might need later. He sat at the tiller and the two Gurkha soldiers manned long bamboo steering poles on either side of the boat. Where the current took them too close to the banks on the bends, the Gurkhas pushed them off.

Kraske looked slowly round the other faces: Sam Jordan, Gail Crawford, Luis Moreno, Kamala Chavan, and Leila Sumantri nursing her baby to her breast. None of them were friendly. They looked at him with disgust or anger, and Leila hugged the baby closer as though afraid for its safety. Only her husband made no response. The Indonesian was either asleep or in a coma on his stretcher.

So Falcon had told them. There had been plenty of time. The sun was high, and from the width of the river and the passing groves of nipa palm and mangrove which had replaced the lofty rainforest Kraske knew they must be approaching the sea.

Falcon handed the tiller to Jordan and came forward.

Kraske watched him, waited for him to speak. But Falcon let the silence saw at the other man's nerves. Kraske finally spoke first.

'You could have left me, Mark. Why did you bring me along?'

'Be thankful I did,' Falcon told him. 'Sergeant Rama wouldn't have left you alive.'

'So what am I? A gift for Western intelligence?'

'No. I just figured I could still use you.'

Kraske looked uncertain. 'How?'

'To get us past Batakan. You see, I figure that to take over Surajong and the upper reaches of the river, then you and Mathias must have some pretty strong support at the river mouth. Your friend Yamin had plenty of time to radio a warning downstream before he left Surajong, so we could be running into another ambush before we reach the sea.'

Kraske licked his dry lips. He didn't want to confirm or deny.

'But I reckon we've already pressed our luck too many times,' Falcon went on. 'So I don't intend to risk another bloody firefight getting through Batakan. That's where you come in. The delta is a maze of creeks on either side of the main river, so there must be a way to bypass the town. You ran guns into this area for the KGB, so you must know all the back ways. You're going find one for us.'

Kraske thought about it. 'Maybe there is a way,' he admitted at last. 'But what do I get in return for this favour?'

'Your skin, in one piece,' Falcon said calmly. 'My word that I'll put you ashore as soon as we sight the open sea.'

Kraske smiled bitterly. 'That's one hell of an offer, Mark. You're planning to put me down in a stinking swamp full of hungry crocodiles. Where there isn't a crocodile I'll be treading on a snake. And if that isn't enough then maybe you should know that the Borneo swamps are the home of the biggest, most dangerous goddamn lizards in the world. The natives call them dragons. They don't breathe fire, but their bite is poisonous!'

'It's still an offer you can't refuse,' Falcon told him. 'Because it's the only offer you're going to get.'

Bahadur Rama was again playing hopefully with the hilt of his kukri. The two Gurkha soldiers had stopped poling for a moment and were watching and listening with close interest.

Kraske scowled at Falcon and nodded agreement.

They had a deal.

It took them three hours to pole through the narrow creeks and branching waterways behind Batakan. They were back in the moist, steamy heat of the lowlands and the mosquitoes buzzed in thick clouds. There were places where the great, tangled roots of the mangroves almost blocked the narrow channels with their intricate archways, and several times they had to use the parangs that were part of the boat's equipment to chop their way through.

They didn't see any of the dragon-lizards Kraske had mentioned, but the crocodiles were plentiful on the mudbanks, and twice they saw pythons hanging in ugly coils from the upper branches of the mangroves.

It was slow, back-breaking work. The steering poles stuck fast in the mud and after each thrust it required an equal effort to pull them free. Twice they had to back out of channels that were blocked and each time Kraske insisted that he had not lost his way.

'These creeks change with every tide,' he pleaded. 'Some of them silt up. Others get flushed clear. The sandbars keep shifting. Even when you know them you can never navigate the same route twice.'

'Just find us the sea,' Falcon warned him.

And Bahadur Rama stroked one hand gently down the scabbard of his kukri.

Kraske was standing up in the prau to widen his range of vision, and to stop him from jumping overboard Falcon had lashed one of his wrists to the mast. Kraske bit his lip, and with his free hand pointed out what he hoped was the true way ahead.

The detour was taking time, and they were all suffering, but Falcon still calculated that it was a better choice than continuing to run the bloody gauntlet down the main flow of the Kiamba. If there was any reception at Batakan they had avoided it completely.

Slowly the great blocks of mangroves and palm trees broke up into large and then smaller islands. The waterways became wider, and at last the curving white cream of the surf line appeared ahead. Behind the surf the green-brown waters of the delta became the bright clean blue of the open sea.

Falcon steered the prau over to a protruding sandbar that ran like a yellow path back to the nearest tangle of mangroves. He used a parang to cut Kraske free, and then handed him the heavy jungle knife hilt first.

'I won't trust you with a firearm, but you'll need this to walk back.' He paused. 'If we had any drinking water I'd give you some — but you know there isn't any.'

'I believe you would, Mark.' Kraske tucked the broad blade of the parang under his arm and rubbed at his sore wrist. He eyed Falcon shrewdly. 'You could be making a mistake. I'm a long way from dead. Maybe we'll meet again.'

Falcon didn't answer.

Kraske shrugged. He glanced round the boat, saw that no one was going to wish him luck, and then stepped over the side. He walked up the sandbar, and then paused to look back from the edge of the mangroves.

'Learn to kill cold, Mark. It's your only weakness.'

He grinned and waved once, then disappeared quickly into the swamp.

Falcon started the auxiliary engine and headed the prau out through the white froth of surf into the Java Sea.

It was late afternoon before *Scotsman* found them. Falcon had hoisted the sail of the prau and tacked back and forth a few miles over the horizon from the coastline. The destroyer was patiently cruising a similar to and fro pattern as Bartlett waited for the expected radio call from the SRN5, and it was only a matter of time before they sighted each other.

When his party had been taken on board the British warship Falcon chopped a hole in the bottom boards of the prau and left it to sink. He went forward to join Bartlett on the bridge, and the destroyer set course immediately for Malaysian waters.

It was over. Some good guys and a lot of bad guys were dead, and the Kiamba was a river of blood. And all for what?

Falcon lay on his bunk and thought about it.

The evil of international terrorism had spread worldwide, even to the most way-out, forgotten little corners of Borneo. It was spreading the way the Black Death had spread in medieval

Europe — a new, malignant twentieth-century virus carried by an even more vicious breed of rat. Everywhere there was a grievance or dissatisfaction — the pathological, self-destructive poison was taking root.

Maybe in a perfect world there wouldn't be any grievance or dissatisfaction. No breeding grounds of hardship and poverty where the new pestilence could take hold. No areas of frustration and injustice which the political wolves of animal man could exploit.

But this wasn't a perfect world. Man kept trying, but so far he had never quite succeeded in finding Utopia. Because always the black forces of the human beast were striving to rule over the less-aggressive majority of the human race, hoping to grow fat, rich and powerful in their corrupt little kingdoms or great empires.

It was the way of the world. As old as the first tyrant. And terror had always been the sharpest sword in the armoury of evil.

The new obscenity of international terrorism, with its sensational, headline-seeking atrocities in which any victim would serve, was just a new twist on an old abomination.

Which was why the weak and the good would always need their own hard-hitting champions. Feudal England had its knights in shining armour. Medieval Japan had its roving *Samurai*. The Old West had its tin star and its gun-toting lawman. All of them with their own code of chivalry and honour.

And the modern world had its White Warriors too. A few men like Harry Killian — and Mark Falcon.

It wouldn't be long before Killian would call again. And Falcon would answer the call for help. Anywhere. Anytime. The arena could be in any part of the world, from city street to desert sands, from jungle wilderness to Arctic waste. Wherever the black forces chose the duelling ground, the Falcon would answer the challenge.

The door creaked open and Gail Crawford came in. She wore a man's bathrobe which someone had loaned to her, and when she slipped out of it she was smooth, white and naked.

The sweet promises were back in her eyes.

'We've been through so much together,' she said huskily. 'It seems silly for us to sleep alone.'

Falcon was naked too. He moved over to make room for her.

'We're heading for Singapore,' he told her. 'Bartlett decided there would be better hospital facilities there than at Kuching. Some more exotic fun-spots for us, too.'

'I can't wait.'

'You don't have to.'

Falcon kissed her. Her mouth was hungry. Her body was filled with relief and longing.

Falcon began to relax, to forget about the next battle. He needed her. She needed him. And even warriors had to rest between the wars.

It was time to think about Lust and Love.

Rest and Relaxation.

Sex and Sweetness.

That was far enough down the alphabet — a good long way from D for Death.

He decided to just concentrate on N for Now.

A NOTE TO THE READER

Dear Reader,

Thank you for reading BLOOD RIVER. I hope you enjoyed reading it as much as I enjoyed writing it. Falcon's new role as a freelance photo journalist means that he is often in the right spot at the right time, and thus broadens the scope for storylines much wider than if I had kept him permanently in the SAS. His old boss is now working for MI5 and frequently calls upon him to use again all his old battle skills. In some missions he can be assigned military back up, and in others he will work alone. Either way you will be guaranteed a thrill a minute action adventure in one of the hottest parts of the globe.

I have written under other pen names and so my website is at **www.robertleaderauthor.com**. Go to **my Robert Charles page** for more information on my Robert Charles thrillers. My website was always meant to be reader friendly, with a full biography, a travel blog and notes on how each book came to be inspired and written. Please pay it a visit if you would like more information on Mark Falcon or anything else I have written.

In today's publishing world online reviews are vitally important and if you have enjoyed my work please spare the time to write a review for **Goodreads** and **Amazon**, or just a complimentary mention on any media platform.

If you want to contact me you can do so through **my website**. I am always pleased to hear from readers. In the meantime I will get on with the next Falcon SAS novel for your enjoyment.

Sincerely yours, Robert Charles

Sapere Books is an exciting new publisher of brilliant fiction and popular history.

To find out more about our latest releases and our monthly bargain books visit our website: **saperebooks.com**

Printed in Great Britain
by Amazon

18652487R00099